A Columnist Looks at Life

HERE'S...

CAL RUTSTRUM

Nodin Press
Minneapolis, Minnesota

A Columnist Looks at Life
by Calvin Rutstrum

ISBN 0-931714-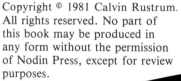

Nodin Press, a
519 North Thir
Minneapolis, M

Printed in USA
Gopher State

Table of Contents

An Introduction

The columns herein are a widely diversified speculation on life as most of us live it, and as I, the author, in my 84 years, also have found it.

Since no effort has been made in the writing to "pull punches," some of the columns may raise a few eyebrows. This is only because today we tend to seek a more realistic expression—becoming less inhibited, less the sedulous ape to convention, less obsequious to the dictates of a materialistic culture and the cults of various persuasions.

The author's lifetime on the whole has been divided annually between city and wilderness.

It has been considered that since the columns herein are sufficiently generic in application to current life and the uncertain future, they ought to be published in book form, where they might throw some light on the existing problems which beset us daily, and perhaps provide a few amenities we could use for greater fulfillment of life, without the author necessarily presuming to be didactic.

Newspaper columnists are not, as we observe, the required precursers in the news media. They come trailing along as a rear-guard action to sum up and digest that which vanguard reporters initially dredge up as current news. Where columnist and reporter differ in occupation is that a reporter is obliged to give names, dates, places and other annotated data of events, while the columnist's need is to draw meaning, effect, consequences, abstractions, and what other analytical substance he can from the press and life generally in its broader reference and personal point of view.

It might be said that the columnist on the whole is more interested in a kind of philosophic, rather than a newsworthy, approach to events—a studied indulgence in principles from which events and ideas evolve.

C.R.

The Best of Two Worlds

Here on the St. Croix River, tucked picturesquely into the valley, is the historic village of Marine on St. Croix. And here my wife and I have our permanent residence, though itinerant we are.

The village has such shops as provide the ordinary needs of life. Now and then an extraordinary need has us reaching for the city but not often.

It is the river primarily that brought us here, one of the impressive ones in the wild-river series.

We passed the village on frequent canoe travel, stopping for fresh supplies or merely refreshment.

We talked casually about the possibility of living in Marine on St. Croix, but this at such times seemed mere fantasy. There were too many inhibitory factors. We were caught in the urban maelstrom of business, content for the time that we could escape to the St. Croix River on weekends.

Two factors were uppermost in our minds. We were convinced that city life did not provide the fulfillment we desired, and the urban environment, we were convinced, was not conducive to optimum health of either mind or body.

Economically I was doing quite well, operating with a partner a small real estate brokerage business in Minneapolis. But in time the repetitive nature of it palled. I saw an uninterrupted eternity of listing property and selling it.

I suppose it is this conventional grind in many fields that sends people to the far-reaches of the earth to explore or at least to somehow reorient themselves.

Early one fall at the most profitable peak of the real-estate business, I gave it up and took a job with the investigative agency of the American Banking Association.

Here at least seemed an escape from boredom. While the tedium of investigation also had its dulling moments, there was always enough periodic challenge to temper it, and give adventure.

In time, finding it an exciting game, I developed a capability in running down absconding bankers and bank robbers. I had been hired on a per diem basis. While it seemed that bank robbery had become epidemic in those days, there were some leisure intervals when I was not busy. My employer required only that investigators be available by phone during these intervals.

I saw in this, of course, an opportunity for some leisure time on the river. As I became more capacitated in criminal investigation work my independence grew. I would head up on the St. Croix River and arrange for some local messenger to find and notify me whenever my office called.

Ordinarily I should have been fired for not being readily available in the intervals between cases. But I had been quite successful, and competent replacement was difficult in this specialized field.

Charlie Brown had a real estate business in Marine on St. Croix, with an office in a small, one-time shoe repair shop. He did, however, have a telephone, and Charlie in his listing of property got around. He knew every hill and dale in the valley, every access road and trail.

When I took off upriver with my canoe and pack, Charlie knew that I would be either on the river in a canoe, or at one of a number of camp spots, usually at known small streams or springs, if my office called. A distant spiral of smoke in the valley was likely my campfire which he spotted from some high vantage point. This went on for several years with the disdain of my employer. When I offered to relieve the situation by resigning, my employer's tolerance was renewed. It was even sustained for a period of two months each year when I headed into the Canadian wilderness on a canoe or dogsled trip.

Charlie's task was greatly reduced one day when he sold me a five-acre tract of land overlooking the valley, within the village limits of Marine on St. Croix. As a hobby I built on this acreage a stone house, using the intervals mentioned of four years, hand cutting and masoning each quarry stone, meticulously fitting each wood member.

That was some forty years ago. The pine seedlings that I carried home in a bundle under my arm, are now a forest on our property with trees of such girth I cannot get my arms completely around them. The stark reality of this time-passing should be made apparent, especially to the young, for the planting of seedlings seems as vivid as though it were yesterday. I wish that I could somehow slow the passage of time— hang onto its coat-tails as I believe Walt Whitman suggested.

When selling hours for dollars the important thing in keeping from being cheated is to know when one reaches the point of diminishing returns. Few make this discovery soon enough, and so barter away much of their lives, beyond needs.

Here at our residence on the St. Croix we awake each morning with the mood of the river valley. Being on a migration route, the flight from and return to the North is our great benefit as it reaches us, the migrant flocks often stopping to feed.

The transition of seasons changes the natural stage-setting and the mood of weather offers something different of interest for almost every day.

Nearby starts the State Park ski trail. Since it needs to be kept clear for ski travel, so in turn it becomes clear, open ground for the hiker. For a mile it skirts what we call the Back Valley; it once, we think, having been the route of the river. Now the Back Valley has become a forest, through which flows a spring-fed trout stream, at one time under the river.

Within a mile the trail dips down into the marshland and spring-bottom of the Back Valley, skirting on high ground the open marsh-water, giving in the course of the trail's meander the luxury of an ever-changing scene. If only all people could hike such trails, would it not be a better world?

Wildlife in the marshland is ever on the move, various species of ducks, red-winged blackbirds and other marsh birds, rise as we approach, and circle overhead, to again light elsewhere in the marsh.

On the trail we meet other villagers, stopping to exchange local news, salutations and comments on the good fortune of having so fine a trail to take our daily constitutionals.

Credo: Seek an anchor-point in some natural area for satisfaction of living, so that you can conveniently greet each dawn from your threshhold with environmental enrichment.

The Open Mind

Each of us must, in varying degree, of course, view life from our own different vantage point. Perhaps our best view of life in general might come from one so completely objective as not to have acquired narrow personal prejudices. Since this is impossible, the contents herein may be said to be a compromise of all things considered.

The open-mind concept can, of course, conjure up some strange nuances of thought. One popular premise is that, if one does not accept whole-hog without question such fiascoes as U.F.O.s coming from other planets; E.S.P. as a sound psychic concept; astrology as a determining process; Big Foot, the Bermuda Triangle, the Loch Ness monster, and other such fiascoes as being valid, one does not have an open mind. In short, the premise here by popular view is that to be gullible of these and other myths is to have an open mind. Rejection of them through lack of concrete evidence becomes offensive to the credulous. Vague presumption is expected of us to be valid concept. As Carl Sagan, the scientist, stated, *"When they present conclusive evidence, I will believe it."*

Should one try to be as intellectually honest as possible in every phase of living, or should one popularly retreat into obscurantism and become the credulous being who comes into the world, accepts the platitudes of convention, myth, and imposed fictions, and goes out as an immediately forgotten entity because of an adherence to mass thinking?

That it is fashionable to be formally stereotyped needs no emphasis. Clothes style is a regimenting process for putting all of us into a collectivist uniform and seasonally changing such dress for the enhancement of the clothing industry. Should our dress not rather be individual, self-styled, attractive, assimilable, and weather-conditioned? Must we be in *"uniform"*, although civilian, to appear well dressed? Run then if you will the whole gamut of advertising and see if there is not an effort to tuck all of us neatly into single national categories for various pecuniary profit, influence, and provincial-minded control. Can this be the hope of a better world, or will the sum total of the best of us as expressed, thinking and choosing individuals, give a greater promise?

The greatest fear of disruption that industry, business, politics, provincial-minded institutions, religious persuasions, and convention suffer, of course, is that we might possibly become a nation of many questioning individuals, demanding of our peers proof of value and authenticity in what is being imposed on us.

The individual has too often been kept in check by being lured with increased salaries from his own individual intellectual aspirations. The professor, for example, who was on some remedial trail of ecology, social rehabilitation, or other aspiring study for good, found the highly increased income for helping to increase the gross national product instead of the quality of life too attractive to resist.

Enlightenment for one or all may thus primarily be a process of individually ridding our minds of much popular opinion. We might perceive by individual thought how popular ascription might be recognized and avoided and how we, as individuals, might set, rather than always follow, a course. The human mind can be so institutionalized as to be limited only to the tenet bars that imprison that mind. You are incarcerated until you question.

The questioning of established authority, whether it be industrial, educational, business, matters of state, particular persuasions, or any other department of human endeavor, apparently has never reached the degree of intensity that it has today. The first impulse of the thoughtful in the examination of this broad questioning has to be concern, of course, about the credibility of the questioner.

Thus, any effort by an individual to treat current problems suffers the question of how objective and understanding can he be? Whether anyone can be objective enough to give more than a compromisingly subjective viewpoint remains ever dominant and moot. Most of us shape our lives by current concepts of human behavior. Any effort to critically examine conventional trends is commonly viewed as an affectation.

In the succeeding columns, an effort will be made to strike to the core of life as best we can, not practice the pseudo-modesty that affected literary propriety has used for parlor parlance. Rather, it could better be stripped bare of pretense— a closer view, into home, office and industry.

Credo: We can afford to be intellectually honest, but this takes initiative, to think courageously and rationally—not act obsequiously.

Criteria, Guide Or Illusion?

What has happened to that host of pseudo-scientists who believed that criteria of the past could be used to resolve the problems of today and tomorrow? We were presumed to learn by example.

On this premise the philosophy of pragmatism was conceived by Charles S. Peirce and William James: the presumption that a course of action has an observable outcome. Essentially this was a study of events and historical phenomena with emphasis on their practical outcome.

How do we equate this with the trend of our present economy? Nothing in the past seems observable to indicate what the result will be from the present inflation spiral.

We have a demand for goods while the Federal Reserve Board has inversely been using such measures as will cut back buying. The law of supply and demand no longer seems to control prices.

To view the problem nationally is to be too limited in our perspective. There was a time when the United States was the focus of industry. The so-called underdeveloped countries were content to sell us raw materials for manufacture. Even the developed big countries were not as industrial as the U.S. so the sale of our manufactured goods had a good market. The world economic situation has now changed. Where forests cut the skyline in earlier days of the underdeveloped countries, now cities and manufacturing mark the skyline.

The world has reached a state of competitive industrial development that ramifies into every country, far beyond what we might presume. Manufactured goods are pouring onto our shores from nearly every country in the world. They tell us that if we do not buy their goods, they will not buy ours.

We face a factor here that is very disturbing to our own economy: a higher quality of goods than ours is competing with our own. This might be argued, but we have to understand that with lower wages in many of the foreign countries, we are competing with a continual effort by the foreign market to produce highest quality of goods for less money.

We in the U.S. have been notoriously guilty of making planned obsolescent goods, to be sold on the installment plan, with the hope that contract purchases at substantial interest rates will keep the average employed individual tied up from the cradle to the grave as a consumer.

Now we face a situation where the fuel shortage and foreign competition will not allow us any longer to flood the market with trashy items. Things will have to be made to last in order to compete. We will be watching imports with a keen analytical eye, in order to compete with them; and we will have to watch the national fuel gauge to see if we can sustain our industry.

We have had much predictability about the length and severity of the recession. If I were to go out on a limb in my prediction, I would be inclined to say that it will be permanent. The same factors of old do not govern the present situation. What we face now is a leveling off that will place the U.S. more on an even keel with the world as a whole industrially.

Our preeminence in the world has suffered. For a couple of centuries we sat on a dominating hill. South Africa now has the nuclear bomb, we are told, as will most every country in time. There will be many *"Jack the Giant Killers"* in the world, where domination no longer rests with the giant nations.

Criteria of the past, thus becomes unadaptable to the future. We will henceforth march by a different drumbeat. Hypothesis becomes conjecture—mere guess as to coming events. With our failure to dispose of waste, pollution and the threat of acid-rain, there is no valid promise that the human race will survive at all. We might accidentally hasten our demise with a nuclear holocaust.

On the other hand the very nuclear imminence that threatens the world could save us. Retaliation always stalks in the offing. We enjoy conquest except at the risk of suicide in the attempt.

There is an imposing outlook that we will soon have to reduce our living standard in order to comply with the needs of the world; more immediately perhaps with the needs of the nation in every walk of life. Where shortages are concerned, nobody is affluent.

If there is one thing I have learned in my 84 years it is that less is often better. On the wilderness trail we find that excess can so encumber one as to make travel impractical. We can likewise encumber ourselves materially on the conventional trail of life, to handicap rather than expedite human values. We somehow fail to discover this fact when we reach the point of diminishing returns. Our materially myopic vision blurs the focus for profound values that have the greatest reward.

Our love for the automobile is an example of how materialism can fall on the ash heap. I watched in a junkyard one day the crushing of cars into highly compressed blocks for the smelter. Nearby was a new-car lot. Soon, I thought, these too will be blocks for the smelter. The true value of course lay in the intangible potential of miles between manufacture and smelter.

Values are much like this in any sense. The future is a nebulous thing—"*miles*" we will travel from now to demise. The vehicles we use to make the trip should not be those that reach the figurative obliterating smelter, but values which can be preserved for intellectual and cultural benefit of others.

Credo: Not criteria alone as a governing factor of our lives, but high aspiration for innovation in a changing world.

The Conformist

Conformism, as it adapts to prevailing social customs and the legislative code, does not seem too far out of order; but when by psychological probe the interloper at large invokes a standard of formal obedience to industrial and business regimentation, it creates a situation offensive, insidious, denigrating, and dangerous in the extreme.

The conformist employer has been continually jittery about the effects of a liberal education. If education follows a pattern of vocational or business development, you have establishment's aid and sympathy—even at times generous subsidy. But a mortal fear haunts the conformist employer that a liberal education based on the humanities, on the liberal arts, on a critical examination of all life's pursuits, impairs the multitude's faith in the regimented, materialistic establishment; risks conventional infidelity.

Conformism has had one of its greatest victories in merchandising, in its skillfully-rigged collectivistic market. Leading psychologists, not averse to their own debauchery if it pays financially, have been lured from great universities at increased salaries to make their "probe in depth" for the purpose of determining the best methods of bringing about customer conformity, induced buying of planned-obsolescent products, deceptive packaging to cheat the customer, and other such chicanery. Mass-mindedness, they know, brings mass sales of unneeded products. Individualistic determination of purchase and discrimination of product imply and demand quality-choice, which precludes the more profitable, stereotype, shoddy items. The appoximately trillion dollar gross national product based on highly-advertised regimented buyer schemes testifies that, in the buying public, individuality and critical selection have been quite thoroughly destroyed. The very high quality machine or custom-made article of artful design, permanence, and traditional pride of ownership has practically disappeared from the market. Planned-obsolescent products drive customers en masse to the market, to the sales contract office at short-spaced intervals—the cycle soon to be repeated.

In earlier industrial history, individualism was highly recognized. It was the individual's innovations, inventions, and proliferation of improved method and imagination that gave the nation in its infancy impetus, and exalted the individual himself. Individualism today is largely obscured by the corporation, or the corporation usurps whatever individual expression its employees manifest, with little, if any, exaltation of the individual or allowing the individual just compensation for idea.

Today, for example, if an employee has individualistic ideas, let him be sure not to feature them as his own. If such ideas are industrially creative, they must become the collective result of the firm's "team research" department. Ideas are not to be regarded as the property of the individual who conceives them. Courts are crowded with cases where employees who have resigned or were discharged are sued even for utilizing ideas which they conceived subsequent to their employment by the litigant firm, the purported legal interpretation being that the nuclei of their subsequent ideas were derived from the essence of knowledge gained in the previous employment. A Thomas Edison today would most likely have to lose his identity completely in the collective aggregation of the individual-obscured industrial laboratory rather than functioning independently—so masterful and cunning has the conformist autocracy become.

The trillion dollar gross national product stands as proof that where our economy alone is concerned conformist tactics have paid off dollarwise, but at the terrible expense of dehumanization and lost ennoblement of individual life—obviously a serious national loss because, on the inequitable basis described, much originality is never revealed. The team-captive inventor divulges only enough idea to maintain his job at top level, scarcely ever at a prodigious level, where he might be the preceptor for a better world.

Enterprise has an element of novelty and interest about it in its inception but in time its repetition palls. Where individuality has been drained out of life by mass production media, the victim tends to become psychotic. It is evident by the growing restless discontent. A certain percentage of the world's individualistic element, of course, refuses to accept the degenerating mandates of conformity.

An aristocracy based primarily on a pattern of business, industry, and conformism has done so well, we are led to believe that it must continue as a tradition. *"The son must follow the father's footsteps. It is the doorway to utopia."*

Unfortunately, however, for such conformism, there is genetics. There is even the rebellious hippy and the questioning new generation to upset conformism. The aristocratic Babbitt father and the socialite mother have at times produced a strange product in the crib. It is known as atavism. The baby is showing signs of not responding to pattern. Grandma says the youngster doesn't look like the father or the mother, nor even a composite personality of the two. She says that a psychiatrist wouldn't be of any help in character analysis at so young an age, but she herself would make a test. On the index fingers of the baby's hands she puts a tiny dab of syrup and adds a single small feather, then stands back to watch. The baby reaches for the feather with the alternate hand and finds that it sticks to a finger of that hand. The baby then reaches for the feather again with the original finger. This goes on several times when finally the baby puts the feather into its mouth and spits it into the crib.

"That baby," says Grandma, *"is an individualist; other- wise it would have amused itself all day, moving the feather back and forth from one hand to the other,"* in the traditional conformist manner.

Credo: Run not with the lemming into the sea of oblivion, but with your imagination to promising horizons.

The Individualist

The individual who seeks a way of life deviating at all from the conformist principle of established order is perhaps the most bedeviled of all human beings. The single white chicken in a dark flock, or the single dark chicken in a white flock, is likely to be pecked to death. An individualist can, I suppose, be anyone who has in any significant degree, by creative accomplishment or innovative thought, removed himself from the perpetual conformist attitude.

One could, of course, argue that individualism, while normally a commendable quality, could apply to the street bandit or absconding bank president, as well as to the imaginative individual with a natural disposition logically, ethically, and independently to think out solutions to his own and such general problems as would react to the advantage of the society in which he lives.

Neat categorical definitions of the individualist are thus not readily applied. Nor can we in all fairness accept the premise that conformists on the whole are necessarily devoid of individualistic tendencies. Some are individualistic but conventionally captive by economic, political, or social circumstances where they cannot without severe penalty exercise their own disposition. Obviously, variations exist in the intervening spectrum between conformist and individualist. But the danger of identification here is that the conformist, no matter how stereotyped, will lay claim to a stable self-determination based on the theory that beyond his "individuality," he is merely being conventionally responsible, where in truth this is not the pattern of what he is, what he is likely to be, nor what most often he is capable of effecting.

The individualist, if he has any autogenous qualities at all, will most likely be the first to recognize his social responsibilities without wholly surrendering his individuality in the process, because he will analyze the substance and merit of these responsibilities before subscribing to their tenets. Or, he will attack these tenets when he is under their mandate if he believes them to be unjust or inane. He is thus apt to go way beyond the conformist in the value of his social responsibility since he will endeavor to improve the lot of humanity rather than follow blindly the precepts laid down by a not always acceptably established order. Unity in a society, for example, should certainly not suggest uniformity or monolithic coalescence. We hear glibly stated that all of us are individual in varying degrees—obviously said to hide the bromidic accommodation that goes with material success. Let there be a strong individualist among us who rears his head with skepticism and a critical examination of existing tenets, one who upsets the common, conformist belief, and you will see the mob defending the status quo with an irrational, unethical, and militant defense. Let the day come politically when a progressive candidate rises out of the static mess and asks for drastic change and improvement—a man who has become restless and impatient with the tragic conditions that surround him—and you will see a clamoring to keep things as they are, lest there be a mil rise in taxes, or any progressive legislative change to disturb the mass routine and belief.

It was the individualist who, down through history, was brutally persecuted and tortured by the conformist multitude, for venturing free thought. It was the individualist who in every sense all the way down through the ages has generously led the conformist mob out of its morass of ignorance.

But there is also the individualist who has by his very individualism brought upon mankind a great misery. There are individualists, for example, who have instigated ideas of rankest, fictional fallacy and persecution, of tyrannical political ideologies, of mechanical excessiveness that befoul the earth with *"improvements"* that destroy our natural environment—those who instigate mass-mind codes that inhibit intellectual freedom, and so on.

Obviously, we need a special kind of individualist, one with integrity, imagination, and magnanimity; one less obsessed with dollar fever, if we are to make the world more livable.

When the Federal Deposit Insurance Corporation (FDIC) Act was proposed, bankers almost en masse looked with horror upon the political *"resectionist"* cutting into their methods of conducting questionable business. Dishonest bankers saw their opportunities of investing in wildcat schemes or manipulating funds seriously curtailed. When we look back on this tragicomedy of banking affairs and note the final result, we find that the honest banker, timorous of change, is now en masse so highly pleased with the security of his position through the FDIC, he rushes to national bank conferences whenever he can to extend the insurance coverage limits on bank deposits and uses the FDIC as his most valuable advertising medium.

It is simply another salient case of the mind of the imaginative minority becoming in slow time the mind of the obtuse, static majority and, therefore, proof of an indispensable need for the creative individualist and an extension of his freedom in any progressive civilization. What bankers thought to be a curse visited upon them by the individualist in the FDIC, they now find to have been a blessing.

Articles which have appeared lately in the leading magazines on Medicare show that the conformist multitude making up the American Medical Association, who so bitterly fought Medicare, have discovered their position greatly improved by the early individual advocates of Medicare.

As one of the speakers at the American Camping Association's Annual Conference, I expressed a regret and challenged that our youth camps and schools by the all-day regimentation program were tending to stereotype our ascending citizenry rather than make of them enterprising individuals. At that time I was under contract as a wilderness activity director with a large affluent midwest group of youth camps, where the president of the American Camping Association at that time was the owner.

He challenged my point of view by asking me to take a group of campers from the organized camp into the Northern wilds where I had a wilderness base and allow this group of young campers free movement.

After this program was carried out, the young campers returned with an added maturity that surprised the camp management.

"Yes, fine," they said, *"but you had a select group of young lads whose behavior and responsibility could be depended upon."*

The next season, to meet this rebuff, I took a group that might be designated as somewhat incorrigible. Their incorrigibility, I found proved largely to be a manifestation of individuality, rebelling against what had been an environment of strict discipline. Their behavior, through the experiment, proved more responsible and mature than the select first group. They had greater initiative, more imagination, greater innovation.

Two of the boys asked to camp alone on an island. They were allowed to select and buy their own provisions and maintain their own program. I made it a point daily to pass the island in a canoe at some distance, seeing them through field glasses, but made no effort to go ashore unless hailed by them to pay a visit. The first few days they ate largely sweets and unbalanced food, I learned, but within a week, of their own accord, they were buying and eating substantial staples. Their clothes, as Robert Service termed in one of his poems, were *"glazed with dirt."* In time, they washed them by going swimming with their clothes on. I humorously chided them about their not too fastidious habits; however, I issued no orders. By the end of the camp season, they were fairly good campers and with moderately clean clothes.

That was in 1946. Today, both of these individuals hold prominent positions in research. To suggest that they achieved this initiative by the fact that in their youth they were allowed a share of individuality would, of course, be mere speculation. To consider that they might have discovered the intellectual invigoration of being on their own by having given them continued leeway may not be speculation.

Credo: Only in the individual lies prodigiousness. It is not a product of the mass mind.

Provincialism

It is difficult for most of us to expand our scope. We become indigenous to a particular religion, politics and environment, and therein usually lies the compass of our lives.

I once knew a man who suffered a kind of claustrophobia on being confined after a lifetime on the prairie to the forest area of southern Canada during his vacation—getting relief only when he could look out upon a large expanse, across one of Ontario's hundred thousand or more lakes.

I was sorely beleaguered in a letter by a reader of my books for not regionally addressing myself to his particular part of the country, an area I thought rather austere, which for the sake of decorum I will leave unnamed. Perhaps the austerity was in my mind, not in the disadvantages of his region. Sentiment, we can assume, has strange bounds.

Recently, I talked to the editor-in-chief of my own state university press, inquiring into the scope of their publication. I had been considering that I might avoid the recent complications of large publishing houses that seem to be falling apart at the seams from imposing costs, increased book prices, and publication policy in general. Some, I learned, now pile up back-orders before reprinting, which is death to authors.

I found that my own world which I thought was quite narrowly circumscribed was of too great a domain for the university press, if they were to publish any of my books. They wanted books largely on their own state and preferably annotated. That annotation leaves out a vast horde of subjects—most of the interesting ones.

Provincially I thought of the man who was invited by an affluent friend to make a companionable trip to Europe—all costs paid. The invited guest appreciated the generosity but said that he had not yet explored his back yard.

There may, on the side of provincialism, be merit in being a "*big shot*" in a small town, rather than a small one in a big city, were it not quite well determined that no prophet is a hero in his own bailiwick. The age-old epithet that "*familiarity breeds contempt*" has obviously not lost its social stigma.

Provincialism is not necessarily confined to geography. It can, of course, be of the mind as well.

Recently the American Medical Association tussled with overspecialization as against an holistic approach to medicine. With the great advance in clinical hardware and drugs, it seemed that nobody with a certificate in the basic sciences could be expected to digest the whole clinical fare. Thus to each his own province of specialization, they reasoned.

To use a biological metaphor, when it was discovered that the Eskimo boy's feet suffered more from the cold when the hood of his parka was thrown back, the holistic concept was given emphasis. A pain in the stomach may be the result of mental anguish, not today's dinner.

Clinical provincialism thus has gradually been turning to the family physician, who has been given back the whole patient body for diagnosis to find the regional problem.

We see provincialism especially prevalent in politics. The Congressman goes to Washington, presuming to have a national scope, and finds that he cannot get re-elected unless he caters to those special interests back in his own district. So he does not become the magnanimous statesman of his own self aggrandizement, but the deferential politician, obeisant to those seeking personal gain. Even a president is plagued by the provincial Sword of Damocles that hangs over him. Special interests dog his tracks at the expense of the nation.

When the continent was first explored, provincialism was the order of the day. It was not until Lewis and Clark probed the continent that the provincial-minded saw fit to burst their geographic bonds and seek new enterprise.

Perhaps it was the inescapable tendency toward provincialism that brought the division of states. Now we have that provincialism in conflict with nationalism.

It is just about the only outward manifestation that distinguishes Republicans from Democrats, although I could suggest some other distinguishing features. As one Democrat told me, *"If Republicans had their way, the borders of states would be fortified."*

In Quebec, we have a current problem where its provincialism desires to cast the advantages of dominion to the dogs. As a French-speaking province, surrounded by an English-speaking population, Quebec with a population of French-English inbreeding through marriage, inconsistently seeks independence as a wholly French-speaking nation. May I rush to the defense of that rational French population who think otherwise, however.

There is nothing paradoxical about this. People of similar origins band together as though they feared that if they did not hang together, as the saying goes, they would hang separately. The very principle of genetics, they should be told, would make their offspring and their whole aggregation better humans by mixing.

I challenge anyone to show that provincialism was and is not a deteriorating factor.

Credo: Leave the village, ward, state, and nation of your mind, until you find a universal rationalism. For—unless you do—you are intellectually stied, cooped and fenced.

The Fallibility Of Predictions

Predictions—more specifically, prognostications—whether scientific or common, are bound to amuse if we think abstractly about them. Computers of late have been relied on to use criteria of the past as input to determine what the future will bring. On this hangs a great deal of irony and improbability.

We speak, for example, about the threat or desirability, whichever, of exponential growth. Before the factor has reached the predicted exponential peak or saturation point, so often some inhibiting factor enters to stem the progress, the acceleration of growth, or whatever the situation happens to be.

We feared, for example, a population explosion, when along came the contraceptive pill for women, and, recently discovered by the Chinese, a contraceptive pill for men. In complement, these pills should dispel the notion that some day the earth will have standing room only.

Environmentalists have feared exponential growth of industry. Here the sudden threat of oil depletion has obviously dispelled the utopian industrial dream of inexhaustible resources for an unlimited number of consumers. The fortune-massing-at-any-cost syndrome has apparently encountered its first major obstacle of illusion.

When you observe industry and the consuming public going materially hog wild, there should be no qualms when you see the vehicle of extravagance foundering. The oil shortage, while scaring the hell out of many people, may in the final analysis prove to be a blessing. Less can sometimes mean more, where human values become the measure of life.

I was pleased when the Supreme Court legalized abortion, largely because I didn't see any justice in having women become legally compulsory incubators. Add to this the late innovative contraceptives and one suffers less about an exponential rise in fecundity and its dire consequences.

When an urgent appeal was made for population control and the need was largely disregarded, what essentially can we depend on as an alternate curb to save the world from ravage and degradation, from over-population—curbs other than the horror of war, highway deaths, cancer, heart attacks and such fatality down the list?

The nearing end of an oil supply may be one answer to this question. If there is such an end, which we are told will occur in about 30 years or less, it could be another factor in curbing the exponentially feared population growth.

Commonly we tend to think of oil for our cars. But there is

the by-product fertilizer and numerous other products. Lack of fertilizer could so affect the food supply as to make the world tenable for only a very limited population.

Where we as humans fail to control conditional runaways, nature seems to stem their exponential growth. Growth-and-decay as a cycle seem to operate successfully to keep the natural world in check. If only humans had the wisdom to operate on such a system, or at least cooperate with it.

Criteria do not give us much to operate on in planning the future, since inadvertence for the events of the moment sets no valid basis on which to predicate coming events. We ran into the oil shortage, for example, like lemmings rushing pell-mell into the sea.

Where extravagance and avarice are condoned as propriety, we are obliged to pay the penalty. Greed, tragically, has been fashionable, but not civilizing.

Today was yesterday's future. Tomorrow will have the retrospection of today. As we contemplate these chronological facts we get some idea that in a finite world we cannot live only for the moment; but we have done so both to our astonishment and regret, perhaps even to our peril.

I have a revulsion in my writing for using didactics. Editors sometimes refer to it as *"preachy"*. Yet, what can we say about the finite nature of things except to state unequivocally that our oil-depletion has been caused by insatiable greed, by indirection, and shortsightedness. What disturbs most is that at the lowest point of an attenuating oil supply, we continue the same extravagant blunders.

Preaching be damned. It's a fact.

At the foot of the exponential curve (note the shape of a cowbell) you will see a gradual rise in the bell's curve. Then suddenly the rise is radically upward. At the top of the bell the exponential curve turns rapidly inward.

The symbolism here is significant. Our whole economy and much of our way of life tend to simulate this radical upward curve, not with concern about the inevitable cut-off.

When we thus operate exponentially we soon find our program curbed, as we have found in the oil depletion and in some other instances, such as the devastation of our forests. Clear-cut and multiple-use of forests end in an ecological tragedy. It is the exponential curve all over again.

Credo: There is a haphazard way of life, and we can presume a prudent way. In time—perhaps generations from now—a people will be born into the world who do not assiduously continue to practice our mistakes. We have a need for innovation.

Are We Running Amuck?

The United States Government has just relaxed the air pollution standard requirement of cities. It is an admission of defeat in trying to make life viable in cities—a poltroonish surrender to those industries which find human values the least worthwhile to greater pecuniary profit if they can pollute and ravage.

Cities are in trouble. There is a notable migration of late from cities to small towns and country because of the already intolerable air pollution conditions.

Professional people are accepting reduced salaries in smaller communities to avoid the din and smog. So, the government presuming to improve economic conditions in the city by relaxing the pollution standard, has made the problem worse.

The five acre tract near a small town has become the most attractive residential choice in the migration trend from the city. Here can be found fresh air, the song of birds, the garden, and a touch of wilderness—that wilderness which Thoreau so aptly referred to as *"preservation of the world."*

There are on the whole of life's future some discouraging and some encouraging forces to consider. As we use up the oil, we must gradually turn to substitutes. One of these is coal. As its use increases so does a consequent, destructive element called acid rain. You have an example of this around Sudbury, Ontario, Canada, where the vegetation is gone, the area resembling a moonscape. The fear now is, that with the increased use of coal industrially, and soon perhaps domestically, a broad destruction of vegetation might occur over the entire county, even over the world, as many of the underdeveloped countries become industrialized and, by using their vast coal supply, begin polluting the air with added acid rain.

Some scientists express doubt that the burgeoning industry in the world will environmentally allow the human race to continue to exist indefinitely. The ocean ports of big cities are so encumbered with sewage and waste, those who upset in small craft tend to meet death by poisoning and suffocation from solids, not only from drowning. Even those who fall into such *"water"* momentarily and are immediately pulled out, are still survival risk cases and have to be hospitalized.

Floating debris and island-like areas of pollution have been found long distances from land, even in mid-ocean.

What has driven the pollution control agency to lowering the standards they say, are the complaints of industry that it costs too much to maintain cleaner standards. Or can we suspect other reasons? Apparently human health and life are more expendable than extra dollar profit.

The arguments presented by industry are that in order to keep prices down there must be less pollution restriction overhead costs. What actually happens where regulation is relaxed is that prices are not reduced, rather they are currently increased, any gain being added profit, the public bamboozled. Will we have a price decrease now? Don't bank on it.

The cost for maintaining a low, current pollution level in industry would be very much less than the bill will be later, when the accumulative situation becomes so over-whelming, correction likely cannot ever be achieved on the basis of the cost it will entail. We have already reached a saturation point where there seems to be no hopeful recourse to save humanity from soon experiencing pollution catastrophe.

We have had endangered species and also species that have become extinct. There is no truly logical reason why the human species might not suddenly find itself pollution-wise in a non-reversible state, where it too may become extinct.

So much for the discouraging aspect; how about the encouraging aspect? This is a subject I have addressed myself to in another column, resting strictly on the hope of an attenuating population. Inflation has made even the two-offspring family untenable, so that now, fewer babies are born. This is a highly encouraging outlook for saving the world from catastrophic pollution. Many schools are closing for lack of students. Contraceptives have been so improved, a distinct reduction in population is now becoming evident. This improving contraception is the most manifest reason, of course, for an attenuating population. The legalizing of abortion also adds greatly to control of population growth.

To point up the amount of waste and defecation produced each year by each individual, merely gets lost in ambiguous figures so I avoid them. Enough to say that a nation of 220 million people produces a mountain of it annually, with no place to put it. Suppose you store in your house daily the total accumulated excreta and waste of your family, you would get an idea in a few years, or sooner, what the earth's disposal problem is in trying to tuck away its excreta and waste from four billion people, when recycling is frowned on by most industry.

Those who avidly rant about pro-life, let them tell us something about disposal that is not just rhetoric and emotion.

What encouragement then do we have?

Only with the population actually attenuating is there hope

for a viable world. Succeeding generations have a chance of seeing the population so reduced that the rectifying processes of nature which work constantly to restore itself from ravage could have a good chance to catch up.

I believe it was the State of Oregon whose governor advertised, *"come and visit, but do not stay"*. Our civic group and not too astute politicians keep talking about *"industrial growth"* when the prevailing industrial and judicial stupidity already threatens to drown or otherwise annihilate us in our own filth and waste.

Preservation of the world cannot have hope with the low intelligence currently exercised but with the shrinking population, once it has moved along far enough to reduce the human count geometrically, we perhaps will begin to see a refurbishing of the world by natural forces alone.

Credo: Let us at last recognize that our greatest obligation is not to personal aspiration, to cult or even to country, but to the preservation of the world, for if we destroy natural phenomena, then all is lost.

Redundancy

In the industrial world redundancy would mean—where honesty is the mode—to make something of such strength and quality that it exceeded standard construction—an article of permanence as it were.

In commercial air transportation, we rest more comfortably seated up in the atmosphere, moving at high speed, if we can be assured that the mechanism had a measure of redundancy over and beyond what ordinarily might suffice to maintain the flight. We have seen of late, jet motors breaking loose, causing catastrophic death.

Planned obsolescence has been a curse upon the consumer, which now, with the shortage of fuel has become an even greater curse. A product so constructed as to last twice or ten times as long, would have saved the fuel unnecessarily burned to make many shoddy items. It is also in the oil shortage where our dishonesty is coming back to roost. Ethics would have made a difference.

My Chevrolet Surburban car, now having been driven only about twenty-five thousand miles, has a body rapidly rusting out. A little better alloy would have saved a share of fuel needed to replace it. The additional commercial under-coating which I had done when the car was new, was not sufficient additional protection to give the body resistance to rust. Muffler and pipes have been replaced twice from rust—all which has consumed additional fuel to mine the ore, make the parts and assemble them. A better alloy is needed in all those parts which rapidly deteriorate.

One hears the remark that deterioration is what manufacturers want, in order to increase sales. If so, these manufacturers have the same moral standard as the hoodlum who gets his loot at the point of a gun.

Recently there have been some TV commercials featuring redundancy—a step up, that is, in quality exceeding what is barely standard, which still usually means inferiority.

One firm made high quality tools and small power units. Among skilled craftsmen these products were known and highly praised. Then came items by a firm making fine appearing products but of minimal service use. The company making the quality items had to adopt a low grade line to compete. They still make the quality items but it is a small percentage of their lesser quality line.

If there is an industrial collapse from lack of fuel, it will be the planned obsolescence element who should accept a large part of the blame.

Obviously the whole industrial process rests on getting more intelligence into commerce. Greed without intelligence or industrial honesty can be a vicious combination. It is difficult to convince the low-minded that it is the long-haul quality item that is important in resolving much of the world pollution problem. Ephemeral product industry sees the tragedy of planned obsolescence but being short of foresight does nothing toward a solution.

High-minded industry resolves its own problems. The low-minded need legislative bans and direction.

Redundancy as defined by exceeding what is barely needed to get by—raising the quality of everything for safety and economy of finite fuel—could be the trend that might save the world from industrial collapse.

We might also be a bit redundant in our ethical approach—avoid pinchbeck standards, extend service to backup failure when it occurs.

In my youth we bought milk from a bulk can. Most groceries gave measure and then tossed in a few drams to please the customer. We might, figuratively speaking, add a dram or two to everything we do. It might make the carpingly stingy a bit unhappy, but even they might discover the advantage in time.

Credo: Lift your opponent as in football up off the ground after tackling him. We, too long, have been kicking the prostrate consumer.

The Old Versus The New

The old versus the new? Some of us well along in years suffer a certain nostalgia for the old. *"The good old days"*, we call them. But some of those days were not so good.

We died for want of penicillin and other antibiotic drugs. Tuberculosis ran wild.

I remember when the work week was six days, and each day was ten to twelve hours. I remember the sweat shops and the mines where death often came around at the age of 35 to 40. I remember when there were no benefits to be derived when you were unemployed, and there was no social security. If you got old and had no backlog to keep you going, they sent you over the hill to the *"poorhouse"*, as it was called.

I remember when the so-called *"cop"* was referred to as the *"mick"*, who thought he was police, prosecutor and judge, though on occasion you would find a kindly considerate spirit among the imperious, plebeian horde of police.

I could go on; there are many such things to remember. Or should we say to forget?

We might remember that hamburger, bacon and ham were ten cents per pound. A hundred pounds of flour, labeled 98 pounds to show that two pounds might be dusted out through the cloth sack from handling; cost, 98 cents. Milk was 4 cents per quart, then sold in bulk. You brought your own milk pail, or other container.

These prices seem beyond belief. But wages were correspondingly small.

You could buy a two-bedroom bungalow, lot and all for $3000. An $8000 house placed you in the bourgeois income group, where you could employ a house-maid for $3 per week plus *"keep"*.

I bought a new Model T Ford Roadster for less than $300.

A daily newspaper cost a penny. The Sunday edition cost five cents.

A nickel took you by streetcar to anywhere you wanted to go in the city. From the ends of the lines you could soon on foot be in the wilds.

I got two pork chops, fried potatoes, bread, beverage and pie for twenty cents.

There was no income tax, no parking meters. Fifteen cents was the admission to the Unique Theater on Hennepin Avenue, Minneapolis, where you saw a whole vaudeville bill.

I don't remember teachers striking in those days. I don't remember the city having any trouble paying the educational bill, the garbage removal, the snow removal, etc.

Farmers went along on a basis of crop production or failure. They didn't complain. Food prices were based on supply, but always very low. Farmers seemed independent and happy.

You could get people to work, whether white collar or common labor.

Am I painting too rosy a picture? Perhaps. There were, no doubt, flaws in much of what I have said, but on the whole I have hued fairly close to the line.

What has gone wrong today? We have a high unemployment rate. But try to get some help to mow an acre of grass, cut brush, remove snow from a roof, dig a garden, and you find difficulty.

Farmers cannot raise a crop and make it pay. Labor and material are too high for people to buy homes; interest rates have gone wild. A recent report showed houses so poorly built, they are a safety hazard. A tornado pulls every nail, piles the kindling. I saw plywood sheathing applied with half or less the required nails.

We can talk about shifting economy, costs, inflation and the rest of the abstract terms, but viewing the old and the new, I see in recent years an unmitigated greed, coupled with dishonesty. We have seen political demoralization, industrial disregard for health standards, and a worse disregard for environment that affects the health of everybody. There is a desire to ravage every natural area. Timber companies want to clear-cut forests; that is, cut everything for convenience of operation. The natural areas must be turned to multiple use, the timber industry tells us. Log-off, graze, hunt, build roads, mine, until there isn't a sign of wilderness or wholesomeness remaining.

Plunder hadn't reached all the area in earlier days. There was room for the human spirit to expand, values to grow.

We have not become sufficiently civilized to discover that we are rapidly becoming a nerve-shaken nation, that wilderness is a necessity. As John Muir pointed out, we need an *"awakening from the stupefying effects of over-industry"*. Most every urban resident is in one degree or another plagued.

Earlier in our history we did not have to seek the remote patch of wilds. It was almost at our doorstep. If we make here a single comparison with the later days, surely life earlier had at least a wholesome approach. By circumstance and smaller population we were inadvertently couched in the very lap of nature. Now we have to search for it, fight for it.

As we read history we have wondered how whole nations could possibly collapse from corruption. The utterly stupid inflation spiral of late tells us that we, the boasted democracy of all times, may be heading for some point where we can have only diminishing returns. The old days had their shortcomings, but did they hold the uncertainty we have now?

For the first time in history economists predict and hope for a devastating depression.

Credo: What goes up must come down by gravity; in economics, always with a crash. The important thing is wise salvage, not despair. But this takes altruism, our rarest commodity.

Our Muddled Economy

We might presume that there are profound intellectual solutions to most problems, but how much intellect as compared to dull conformity is usually applied to the problems that beset us daily?

Our scope needs to be universal, not provincial. Those countries which a few years ago were almost primordial, now have become industrial, looking for markets and world influence.

We, here in the Untied States, are striking out desperately for markets that do not exist. Japan wants us to buy their industrial overload; the United States expects Japan, in turn, to provide a receptive market for our excess.

Planned obsolescence for many years ran riot, filling warehouses with shoddy merchandise, but competition eventually compelled us to quit making poor merchandise—items with a beautiful enameled patina on them to fool the buyer. Japan competitively brought our industry out of this nefarious industrial slough by their government making it mandatory, in cooperation with industry, to stop planned obsolescence and export from Japan only quality goods. As a result, Japan practically monopolized the camera business and the manufacture of other high grade technical equipment. Lately, we have refurbished our own somewhat industrial obsolescent goods, but we have a long way yet to go to get out of the planned obsolescence kind of economy. A shortage of energy may see to that.

All of what I have said, of course, is mere industrial flamboyance. What I'm leading up to is a matter of intellect in our economy. I'm certain, however, that much applied intellect won't work—not because it is basically wrong in posture and won't resolve problems, but simply because people on the whole have a morbid fear of intellectuality. They have confidence in a plodding mediocrity. They don't, for example, vote for highly trained, brilliant economists; they prefer a homebody on their own intellectual level, who they think is down to earth and understands their problems.

Obviously, he doesn't.

We have in the United States about ten million people unemployed. This means (if we are to judge by our current method of doing things) that in order to dig a ditch requiring ten men, you are supposed to work the hell out of nine, so the tenth can sit on his butt and draw relief.

Intelligence would tell us that the nine of us would not have to work such long, weary hours digging the ditch, if we could get the tenth bench warmer back to work by our providing a job for him through a wise distribution of labor.

An intelligent remedy would be simply to ask that the working week be reduced to 4½ or 4 days, so the bench warmers could fill a resulting labor shortage, incurred by all of us working fewer hours.

The proposal would, of course, cause a stampede of industrialists, economists, idlers, economics professors, and a host of others heading for Washington, complaining that distribution of labor would be economically impractical, or simply that it would upset the present routine.

If we think the shorter work-week won't work, let's go back a few years. In my early 20's I worked on a job ten hours each day—12 including overtime—six days a week, and sometimes a half a day on Sunday if the industry was swamped with orders.

When the demand came for shorter hours, there was a whoop and cry that could be heard round the world. *"What will people do with all that spare time on their hands? They'll go crazy,"* industry said.

One thing they did with the leisure time was to add a multi-billion dollar recreational industry to the nation's economy. People began to enjoy a little more leisure. Less weary on the job, they did better work. They discovered in the shorter week the essentials of sunshine, fresh air, and diversions in an outlying natural environment. It was, in a limited sense, a kind of recreational renaissance, which, if expanded now, could threaten to make industry and the rest of us more civilized. Selling five-sevenths of our daily lives each week for subsistence, borders on the ridiculous. If we made higher quality merchandise that lasted, we could pay the same wages and reap the same profit existing now for planned obsolescent trash, provide more leisure and better national health.

When the Indian was asked why he worked only two days each week instead of five like the rest of us, he said, *"I couldn't make it on one."*

Three-day weekends now show up at times during the year when a holiday is included. The recreational advantage in the long weekend is extraordinary, increasing the economy tremendously.

It will not be long, I have come to believe, when every weekend has three days with possibly a fourth added for a holiday. What we need in order to accomplish this is just a slight but active trend toward an intelligent economy.

Credo: Solutions to our economic problems are readily available in the mind's eye, but those who could change things cannot do so with myoptic vision.

The Illusion of Plethora

There is a growing concept that we will be obliged to lower our living standard if our economy is to become viable. What that entails is an interesting subject.

It doesn't mean what it did earlier. You can now have a fat purse and find many things unaffordable. The dictionary defines the term AFFORD as, *"To have the financial means; be able to meet the expense of"*.

Lexicographers please note: You will have to change this definition to meet the new standard.

We have suddenly discovered that we have a finite supply of world goods. If you are rich—and I hastily add, since you are of ethical responsibility—you won't indulge your affluence. You will buy only what is essential to your needs, so that your fellow citizen can equitably supply his.

The concept of a lower living standard as a whole is staggering to contemplate. Heretofore, material pretension was considered the earmark of superiority. You could decorously flaunt your possessions; now you may find the disdain of your peers if you have more of the world's goods than you need.

To achieve distinction earlier, what you needed most was money. Since most of the population had the same aspiration, though in varying degree, your pecuniary level was your measure of distinction, no matter what your intellectual or cultural level.

Presuming that all of us are required to lower our living standard, what does this mean? Do the poor become poorer? What about the middle income element and the rich? How do we impose the same world-goods restrictions on all, without serious inequities? Do we continue to build million-dollar homes for pretentiousness alone when there is a shortage of building material due to shipping our cut forests overseas for higher profit?

A reduced standard of living considered in an aggregate sense, obviously becomes a farce. People who have ample means will find products for sale. And the ethical level of humanity is not of that order where the distribution of scarce goods will be equitably allocated.

We hear and read the expressions that *"smaller is better; less can mean more."*

Thoreau suggested that we might for awhile live in austerity to determine what is truly essential for maintaining a rationally viable existence.

On the television program *"60 Minutes"* they featured a

young couple without children, who had a total annual income from two salaries of about 36 thousand dollars, and found it difficult to save an amount adjustable to the future. They took a large part of their meals in restaurants to avoid the problem of preparing them at home. Despite the fact that they required a home for only two people, they were paying on a contract of almost $500 per month. They had saved only $3600.

Had they easily prepared most of their meals at home in micro-wave, pre-timed ovens, and purchased a house in keeping with their needs, they could have added the difference of at least $6000 to their bank account annually.

We can presume from the above that the whole of their $36,000 annual salary, was just as badly handled.

I am reminded of two families in a nearby city. The fathers were custodians in public schools with the same salaries. One family bought on contract an outlying home with an extra lot for a vegetable garden; the other rented a house within the city residential district. One family, the renter, was continually behind; the other paid for the home and extra lot, besides managing a savings account.

One enjoys going to a good restaurant for dinner occasionally, but to have the time-saving facilities of a kitchen in a modern home and scarcely ever use them, then complain about the meagerness of an ample budget, suggests gross incompetence, a sort of luxurious obscenity, and phlegm.

On driving 300 miles to our cabin on the Canadian shore of Lake Superior, we usually stop at a restaurant for lunch. There we drop the better part of a ten-dollar bill, when a couple of home-packed sandwiches and a thermos of beverage, consumed at a park rest-stop, are tastier and environmentally more enjoyable.

If we consider this figuratively, it suggests that most people with ample salaries fritter away their income on nonessentials, that contribute little if anything to their welfare—the old adage of *"penny wise and pound foolish"*.

If we could lower our standard of living in such a way as to de-emphasize pretentiousness of material goods as a measure of distinction, we might begin a new cultural renaissance. Our greed for material things, acquired just to show off—to disparage those less materially affluent, might lessen.

We could liken our material glut to background music in the drama. If the music is in complement, that is, obscure enough so that the drama is prominent, we have a successful presentation. If the music raucously protrudes itself on the drama, all fails. If we are so materially greedy that our culture suffers, we can have no valid boast of civilization.

Material pleasure need not disappear; it need only be the moderated background music to the drama of our cultural life.

The finite condition of the world's resources, suggests that we had better get on with a more economical program, whether or not our avarice likes it. We can't afford economic stupidity.

Credo: Let's resurrect from the grave and use to an advantage, that old cliche that we failingly *"know the price of everything and the value of nothing"*, since it is on this premise that we are constructively able to distinguish between competent and inept people.

The Money Market Explosion

My wife and I have always looked with a polite and respect-ful but nevertheless mild disdain on the dollar market. The financial page, unread by us, was usually the page to wrap the garbage, though with no meaning of offense. What stocks we had acquired came through inheritance; and the accumula-tion of our earnings over and above living expenses went into government bonds or a chance bargain in waterfront real estate.

So, we have not been monetarily rich nor actually poor. Our wealth, we felt, lay more in the serenity of the mind, in the con-templation of human values, the arts and the natural world. When dawn broke over our waterfront we were complacent and provincially undemanding of the business world. When night drew the curtain on the day's interest and occupation, we slept without apprehension of what financial gain we might have gleaned or lost by fluctuation. A functional return of in-terest on our bank deposits and government bonds, con-tributing as it were to what few *"altruistic"* dollars we deposited in the lending money market for farm loans, home mortgages, car and utility buying, kept us perfectly satisfied with the order of things as they functioned normally.

Farming, home-building, business and other utilities requir-ing short-term loans, moved along with the degree of modera-tion and satisfaction that a democratic society could expect. And it seemed that this would continue to be the eternal rou-tine policy of the utilitarian world with only slight variations.

We did look somewhat obliquely at those who sought fulfill-ment of life primarily in material aspiration, fending off with diplomatic nicety those who shared our table and who held the conversation boastfully to a guarded monetary *class distinc-tion.*

So far so good. One morning having received a check from my publisher, we sought routinely to buy another quarterly interest-bearing certificate. Our banker advised us that the in-terest we were receiving on previous certificates had suddenly doubled.

Doubled? I couldn't believe it.

We were now to our dismay caught in the same financial maelstrom of those who find their chief inspiration in dollar adventure.

What about those insurance policies we paid into so generously? Would we not take a financial loss on them?

What about our government bonds? They now, with the explosive interest rates, had sacrificially low interest rates.

What about our savings accounts that we used to bolster our checking accounts, maintained primarily in the event of an overdraft?

What about our stock shares which we had given little regard for except to note the amount of regular dividends?

Moderate as our whole package of investment is, the resolution of it now seemed intricate and subject to alteration.

An immediate switch-over to the higher interest rates would if done before maturity date entail a penalty, so we had to consider balancing this penalty against the new high interest rate gain. For one such as myself who adds a column of figures ten times and gets ten different answers, the task seemed insurmountable. I longed for and still long for the good old days.

But benevolence, fortunately, rides high. My banker and others told us they would make the comparative calculation and report to us when the switch-over from the old to the new rate should most advantageously be made.

I could now, I thought, forget the whole business, and return to our normal way of life, sans finance. But it seemed we were destined by the radical shifting of interest rates to again concern ourselves with the flotsam and jetsam of the financial world.

The old routine seemed so much better, and I would gladly join an aggregate movement to return to it if someone would lead. I felt sorry for people who had to borrow money. In fact I felt like a greedy accessory to their misfortune.

I know farmers who must sell their farms because they cannot pay excessive interest rates. Car dealers and car buyers are in a precarious position where contracts double the price of cars already priced beyond their per-mile value. Homes cannot be bought or built by many where the interest rates on contracts prohibit their ownership.

We wonder how soon small banks will begin to fail where they do not have an ample number of depositors and a correspondingly limited number of borrowers. Thank goodness for the F.D.I.C.

Those who invested in land seem to have acquired the most intrinsic values. I feel sorry here too for those who try to buy waterfront property on which to build a wilderness cabin for diversion from *"the rat race."* Such frontage was somewhat at a premium even earlier, and now has become truly prohibitive for those nature-oriented people with moderate incomes.

Wage and price controls in a free enterprise system get into conflict. As a temporary measure at least they do not seem to work.

The chief difficulty is that an applied intellectuality does not work either, since any application of a direct, drastic logical solution necessarily means deprivation for one group or another. Accustomed conventional avarice also shies from this. No one is willing to depreciate his own lot, not even when it is recommended as an overall aggregate undertaking for the national good.

Yet it should be obvious that we are sitting on an economic powder keg. Unless we can settle back to an equitable balance between wages and prices, a viable interest rate for all average money-lending needs, and a means of maintaining a tenable existence for all income groups, a crash will eventually come— perhaps the sooner the better. At least, so say the economists.

What is strange about this is that the cost of remedying the problem now, would, no matter how drastic, be much less encumbering than picking up the pieces from a major crash. But we have to ask, *"Do we have that much altruistic competence to set things right?"*

Credo: As we journey along, let us take into consideration not only our commendable intellectual achievement, but regard with concern our incompetence as well. It seems inexorably to dog our greatest achievement, because we are not apt to consider its inevitable presence as a constant minus among a presumably intelligent society.

Our Shifting Lifestyle

In the preceding column, *"The Money Market Explosion,"* I have considered at length the bank interest rates.

If we regard this as a mere statistic, what figuratively speaking might seem like heat lightning, is more apt to prove the foreboding of a protracted storm.

The conventional mortgage being an American institution as intrinsic as apple pie, to discourage it is essentially to destroy the very way of life we have enjoyed as a free democratic society. There is no parellel in our history to what is happening now.

Add to the prohibitive interest rate, an oil combine that is making such unheard of profits as to risk the winter survival of the average citizen. Add to this the loss of the small farmer to corporate farm control of our food supply. Add to this the high cost of building materials for housing, due to a shortage caused largely by shipping our cut forests overseas for greater profit. Add to this the attitude of the American Medical Association when some effort is being made to get care to the average citizen.

Are you already tired of adding? The list is long, tedious and frightening. The list could occupy this whole column, but most of it you, of course, already know.

Do you wonder now why some countries have gone over to a slave-state form of totalitarian rule? The tragic choice then becomes less housing, less choice of food, drabber clothes, regimentation, and your voice is shut off to say only what will be tolerated for a regimented, herd way of life.

Our nation has gone along for centuries as a free democratic society, give or take some inequities that are bound to arise. Can we think that it will continue on that democratic tempo in perpetuity? No country has remained static. We live in a constant state of flux. Some countries have collapsed by sheer political and plutocratic corruption. It can happen to us.

What does the present condition portend?

As I see it, we are shifting away from the democratic state to a degree that is disturbing. The oil industry, by its windfall profits, already has much of the public in jeopardy.

We shudder at the thought of too much government control, and shudder as much when there is not sufficient legislative instrumentality to prevent industry from running rampant.

The program *"60 Minutes"* revealed that millions of government dollars are going to the large corporate farmer at low interest rates—even to breeders of race horses—while the small farmer has to suffer exorbitant rates, or no loans at all.

There are, we have seen, two insidious forces at work in the country: one is an effort to reduce us to a totalitarian, plebeian herd; the other is an effort to create an authoritarian state where much of the population is obliged to knuckle under to corporate rule, as we now are compelled to do where windfall oil profits and similar monopoly are concerned.

If we observe what is going on in the world we see that as the authoritarian state increases, rebellion begins. Then if rebellion succeeds, the shift is not back to a free society but to a totalitarian state, which in turn because of its inevitable drift into austerity has to seek help from free democratic, high per-capita-production countries.

We have this as an example in China, where the individual is gradually being released from totalitarian bondage in order that the country can get up on its economic feet. China needs our help.

We in the U.S. inversely are moving into a plutocratic state by a process so gradual and insidious it is recognized only by the astute citizen. Big mergers are taking place in spite of anti-trust laws.

Senator Udall along with others has been concerned with, not only dangerous mergers, but about the buying up of various publications as well by non-publishing interests, placing in suspect control of the press.

One national magazine to which I had contributed numerous articles, objected to my comment on the problems and abuses of clear-cut methods in the multiple-use of our forests. Apparently it disturbed the timber industry.

It seems that the average citizen will be compelled to fall in line with exclusive corporate thinking, or suffer unemployment or other risk.

This is the price we pay for allowing ourselves to be victimized by plutocracy, communism, fascism or some other ideological plague falling upon our free society.

How then can we avoid them and maintain some semblance of a democratic order? Obviously we need to throw out of office the inept and dishonest element.

How do you designate them? It is really quite easy. Swamp with mail any congressman who appears to defer to special interest groups.

Here we may, on occasion, step on some honest toes, but it will eliminate the outright purchase of public office for seating scoundrels with covert subsidy.

Those who hold office must certainly be expected to represent the public weal—the general good—protecting the minority and the individual only where they are being harassed by public or other forces. There are occasions, of course, when the corporation too needs legislative protection, and even subsidy in an emergency, but these should be given careful legislative scrutiny, to screen out the special privilege risk.

As an investigator earlier in life, I can assure you that with varying colors of the political ethical spectrum, we need eternal vigilance and continual political house-cleaning.

When, for example, you see a politician on the floor fighting for the right to impose high-risk, anti-trust mergers, and other monopolies on the public, you can be sure that you have a scoundrel to vote out of office in the next term of office.

Credo: Before we lose our free society, we need to make sure that industry is serving the public rather than exploiting it for excess profit to gain a financial empire; for then both go down to despair in a nation that otherwise could allow both to prosper.

The UNmaking of a President

Following the Iowa caucus, presidential candidates toppled from their precarious political stances like pins in a bowling alley. While the study of each candidate required no intellectual muscle, each manifestly demonstrated an interesting observation of why so many candidates and presidents down through history have fallen into limbo as forgotten entities.

One listens intently for each voice in a debate to give forth at least a scintilla of edifying hope for a nation in trouble, only to find largely a recurrence of the platitudes and obsequiousness that has overshadowed campaigns since time immemorial.

The loud, garish, emotional shouting of platitudes no doubt impresses the plebeian audience, but it makes suspect for the thinking voter whether the candidate is sincere or simply another opportunist seeking office.

Usually the platitudes are thoughtless, unqualified condemnation of the adversary candidate or party, scarcely ever a fair and analytical consideration.

Calm, charismatic, keenly analytic statesmen have been rare. For that reason we have only a few presidents who have stood out saliently in history.

The factors unmaking a president have obviously vexed and confused candidates more than the presumed, popular attributes needed to be elected. In one presidential election the sponsors of the failing candidate said, *"If we could have kept his mouth shut a little longer, he would have been elected."*

I am not presuming that there is a basic wisdom in the electorate's exercise of the vote, since it certainly has inducted into office a share of scoundrels and nincompoops, though surely a few competent, laudable statesmen as well.

Since the plebeian vote is equal in value to the sophisticated vote, and to all others in the medial voting spectrum, no common denominator campaign speech is usually forthcoming beyond the raucous ballyhoo so universally typical in campaigns.

What might inspire confidence could be a moderated, vocal, sincere expression of a long and trustworthy track-record of service in Congress, but we need to ask, *"How often does this come to pass where there has actually been a high, nationally applied nobility of action in public office, where provincialism and a deference to special privilege are not at least in suspect?"*

We do on occasion find such office holders, but their chances of election to the presidency usually are minimal where they have favored high national standards for the good of all, not just a favored few.

Presidential timber can, of course, be found in the private sector among a number of intellectually competent, ethical people. But those private citizens of dignity and high integrity often have a reluctance to casting their lot with the unscrupulous abuses bandied about by a host of political opportunists. Moreover, since the presidency has virtually to be bought by campaign subsidy, the degradation of such subsidy by special-interest groups, looking for influential favor, is not an inspiring thought for responsible people.

Fortunately a few competent people do get into office with enough honest clout and policing to save government from becoming too farcical to function at all, though one wonders how they manage to evade the shysterism.

Theodore Roosevelt, when once in office, found it expedient to legislatively thumb some of his campaign sponsors on the nose who sought special privilege. While this is a bit devious, Roosevelt apparently was not corruptible.

Another opportunity for UNmaking a president, is when you find a candidate trying for self-aggrandizement to quash commendable effort on the part of his adversaries. In the handling of the Iran and Afghanistan situations, for example, the President was attacked, only to find that the voting, security-conscious public, rose in his favor about two to one.

When you find an opponent negativistically attacking everything that his adversary does, you will be on safe ground in considering the attacker as likely to be both intellectually dishonest and inept. Here, wise, fair, analysis of an opponent and his views could bring confidence, though invidiousness—often vindictiveness by the attacker—prevents it.

Perhaps the most important factor in the UNmaking of a president, is to consider the candidate's *"Monday morning quarter-backing"*. If he has been in a subordinate office for some time and has not found his way into the Oval Office to ask a president of opposite party to consider a hazard which he thinks might be facing the nation, you might well make sure that he does not in his aspirations impose his prevarications on you as a fit candidate, for here you have personal political gain placed above country.

Even the not too astute voter is fooled by continual intellectual dishonesty. No politician has a mind so retentive that he can be a chronic liar. His questionable voting record if nothing else, will give him away to the most casual observer. Many politicians haven't somehow even discovered the pervasive, national coverage of television and radio, since they have a provincial contradictory speech varying from state to state.

Some blanket proviso might possibly be printed on the ballot that would enable one at the polls to safely UNmake a president. If he opposes the conservation of our natural resources and favors ravage for profit, you can be fairly sure that he has sold out. If he opposes all the fundamental legislative needs such as: Improvement of our environment, enhancement of education, national health programs, cutting back poverty, appropriations for research; in short, if he places all the ennobling values of humanity on a pecuniary basis and sees life's fulfillment only on a dollar-profit basis, unmake him for president, for here is civilization's worst regressor.

Credo: The UNmaking of a president can be more important than the making of one, if a debauching type candidate represses what gains we have already made in the civilizing process.

Class Distinction

Almost daily one hears the expressions: *upper class, middle class, lower class,* and we utter these categories without the least snobbish qualms.

Why not upper, middle and low income brackets? After all, the categories boast of money—not nobility of character. By conventional standards we are considered upper *class* if we are endowed with wealth; middle *class* if we are somewhere about midway between poverty and wealth; lower *class* if we are poor. (I'm instantly reminded of the many great men in history who, financially poor, have influenced the world.) Lower class?

When we hear about *class,* few indicate what essentially they mean. The eye is myoptically on the dollar. The credit computer ignores everything outside of one's payment potential. If we're deeply concerned about cost, we're simply told by comparison that we can't afford the expenditure. This, as you see, boasts upper *class*—presumes to give *"exclusiveness"* by way of cash alone. It's a hope ostensibly of lifting oneself up socially by one's bootstraps—among a rational society, just as futile.

Therefore, whether rich, poor or somewhere in-between, we are commonly categorized much as you would rate material commodities, depending on the monetary value. We are told by the mercenary that everyone has a price. If we flaunt a relative amount of cash, it is presumed that we can as human beings be bought like hog-feed or tools across the counter—no matter what our status.

As to your true character status, no one is likely to inquire if you belong to a division of people having estimable quality, rank or grade by notable achievement. Seldom will anyone ask if you're a super craftsman with a reputation for fine work, or farmer with high agrarian know-how; if you're a lawyer or a judge with great judicial sense; if you're an accomplished artist, a Metropolitan Opera star, a scientist, a mathematical genius, a critically observant anthropologist, a physician or surgeon of high clinical capability; nor will anyone ask if you render a commendable qualitative service in business or industry. All that needs to be known by common implication is whether you have the proportionate amount of money to place you in an *upper, middle,* or *lower class* category.

What service we render, what magnanimity we impart while alive, and what resulting residual nobility of effort we leave behind when we die, ought to be the earmarks of having lived a mature and fulfilling life. Simply to leave accumulated wealth behind is, unfortunately, too often no more than a self-imposed commentary on greed.

Since time is our greatest poverty, would it not be wiser to sell only enough of life's precious time to acquire security-with-leisure, so as to allow time for the pursuit of profound values?

Those who have sought to destroy magnificent Lake Superior with pollution to gain a wider margin of profit can only live their lives at best in infamy and soon be forgotten; although they too will be regarded while still alive as upper class.

A president who becomes so corrupt that he and his hench-men are driven from the nation's capitol in contempt, will even though nefariously salvaging enough loot while in office, also be commonly regarded as *upper class.*

Is it possible, that we will eventually reach that civilized level where a man's achievement alone legitimately regards him as *upper class*—that is, by sound generic definition: one possess-ing highly commendable attributes beyond the cash register? This, of course, is doubtful.

We can think of many people down through history who *validly* could be considered *upper class. .* For want of space, I name but a few: Lister, Pauling, Thoreau, Edison, Aristotle, Socrates, Bruno, Burbank, Darwin, Jefferson, Einstein, Sweitzer—the list, of course, could go on.

Let's not however, forget that obscure host of less known people, who haven't devoted their whole lives to money, but have nobly served great causes, as well.

I'm convinced that by the recent conduct of the rising generation, the old saying, *"Like father, like son,"* will largely apply in youthful aspiration only where the father has mani-fested a commendably honest service, possibly high meritori-ous achievement or both. In too many instances, what seemed monetarily fine wine as a way of life to the father, has in an im-proving generation been regarded by the son as small beer in life's greater values.

Credo: Ignorance bleeds through the dollar garments of obsession to spoil our appearance.

Uphill Climbers

When we attempt to make categorical divisions of people according to their capabilities, we obviously find complications. But there are generalizations, and one of these is to make a distinction between that human element who find opposition discouraging, and the element who find it a challenge.

When my wife and I remodeled and improved our newly acquired adobe residence on the Pecos River in New Mexico, our plumbing contract brought an employee to do the work who had arthritically crippled legs, diabetes, and other accompanying illnesses. Our sympathy was felt but fortunately, we learned, was not to be expressed. Somehow he didn't seem to be one who felt sorry for himself, nor wanted our pity.

We had other problems to solve on the twelve-acre, irrigated plot on the Pecos, one being the irrigation system—something that might by trade, we thought, come into his occupational sphere. As we pointed up the problem, his first comment toward a solution was, *"That's nothing for an uphill climber."*

Later when I saw him seated on the floor of our adobe dwelling, working with some of the plumbing mechanism—seated to get the weight off his crippled legs—I thought, *"Here indeed is an uphill climber. And here is courage and nobility of mind."*

Since then, when things seemed to go wrong, when obstacles loomed up to the point of only diminishing returns, I told myself, *"This can be the challenge of an uphill climber."*

Nationally I look forward to a president who is an uphill climber, and a congress that gets to the end of political rhetoric and concludes with action.

I like to think of industry and business that do not drag us downhill ecologically.

I like to think that medical research is on an uphill climb to ameliorate more of our physical woes. I am disturbed about that segment of medicine that is seeking exorbitant profits when it has its patient victims at its mercy in hospital beds.

None of us, of course, should escape the need to put our shoulder to the load anywhere, when the pull is too heavy for others. I remember a realistic depiction of westward ho, when the women and even the children put their shoulders to the wagons when the horses struggled to move the load over hard going.

We are never in such a strategic position, any of us, where figuratively speaking we may not in emergency need the help of a neighbor. Independence is a nice concept where we are self-sustaining when all goes well. To be self-sustaining when all does not go well, is certainly commendable. But there can come a time when even the uphill climber, beyond his own best efforts, needs a shoulder to the wheel. That is the time when we ought to become socially responsible.

Perhaps the lowest caste individual is one, who by good fortune or circumstance, has the advantage of extra muscle and affluence, and uses it only to boast of his good fortune—the superiority syndrome, the autocratic boast.

Few of us can be of the Dr. Sweitzer nobility of action but the world could change rapidly for the better if all learned the miracle of supererogation, a word too cumbersome for popular use, meaning to do more than is required by duty or obligation, beyond at least our own personal need. That extra ounce of helpful extension to others could mean a combined national and world power that would move all of us up the hill and into the valley of more contentment beyond.

Fundamentally, I suppose it simply means that all as individuals need to make an effort to be uphill climbers, then give a hand to those who, by misfortune, falter.

Credo: Pick up the broken sword when needed, and help to win a battle.

Senator Proxmire Profile

The Dick Cavett interview of Senator William Proxmire pleased the sophisticated, and vexed the prudish. The bizarre aspects of the profile, such as the Senator washing his underwear in the shower facilities of the Senate, after jogging five miles from his home to his work, greatly disturbed the priggish who still curtsy but no longer think. That the Senator should be asked about his hair transplant had this same element writhing in their shaken propriety.

If by chance you switched channels about the time the Cavett-Proxmire interview was going on, you might have tuned in to the frippery and exhibitionism of a neighboring state governor's inauguration celebration.

When you find a person in high office who has the earthiness to know what life is about, who is concerned about people who sweat under the arms and look for a viable existence under the same government—there statesmanship should begin.

As you observed in the interview, Senator Proxmire's answers were not platitudes. His sense of humor was magnificent, whether he was asked personal questions or queried about world problems, you had forthright answers. He named the times when by his own indictment his judgment was wrong. He was modest about those times when he was found by the test of time to have been right. When questioned about his colleagues in the Senate there was no calumny, but you knew by his general observations that there were distinctions of competency in the Senate, and not always easy fellowship.

What seemed more apparent than anything was Proxmire's intellectual honesty.

How then do you best judge a man? If he jogs five miles to work each day and washes his underwear in the shower and doesn't care if the whole world knows about it—let me guess—he isn't likely to be hiding anything nefarious about his conduct in or out of the Senate.

Since he jogs five miles to work he is, you can be sure, also honest about his physical and therapeutic needs. There is little danger that he will ever have fattening of the body or fattening of the brain. I don't think you could engage him in flaunting himself in pomp and ceremony to get re-elected.

I don't know why he had the hair transplant. If he was a bald-pate he would still be considered a very handsome man. To add to that—if handsome is as handsome does—he need have no qualms about charisma.

Let's face it; he would make a fine president.

We can be sure that within the breasts of all politicians from aldermen to the Senate, each at some time or other has opined the possibility of some day becoming president. Some men have spent their fortunes on the aspiration of climbing step by step to the top of the political ladder, Proxmire gained his position by merit.

How many of the political rank-and-file gain distinction in the body-politic, and how many are lost in limbo? In each succeeding administration you can count on one hand those who might be even remotely remembered. And many decades have passed when not a single noteworthy individual will be remembered except in *"those dusty archives under the desk that nobody reads".*

Some presidents will have an historical niche of sorts, but they can never be truly great. John Kennedy, for example, had great charisma, but could not sway a Congress. He would on the other hand, have made a colorful king. He would have worn the imperial robes with majesty. But there most of it stops. His press meetings were lively and humorous; perhaps I should have said, witty, since humor calls for depth and he was not a profound man. He had the cart before the horse when he said in essence that we should not be concerned with what the country can do for the people, but what the people can do for the country. How wrong! We need a government that can do something for resolving the problems of society as a whole—not in a pecuniarily benevolent sense—but in a legislative civilizing sense.

Coolidge, Hoover, Harding, Eisenhower and Ford, you name them, can be considered lost entities. Nixon should never be mentioned. Truman will get some consideration, but greatness can fall only lightly on his crown.

"Full, many a flower is born to blush unseen and waste its sweetness on the desert air," as literature tells us.

This quotation might suggest what William Proxmire and a few others down through history, have through neglect, been lost to the Nation as possible good presidents.

Senator Proxmire in his magnificent elementariness has much of the Abraham Lincoln qualities. I believe that had Lincoln been in the Proxmire circumstances, he would have jogged to the Senate and nobly washed his underwear in the shower.

Credo: Intellectual humility is too embarrassing for those of low mind. They want a big facade no matter how false.

The Turn Of Events

As we consider the probable eventual course of society, I am reminded of having read somewhere in early history about a contemplative individual who, looking sadly down from a height upon regiment after regiment of soldiers in perfect military array, stated: *"Just think, in a hundred years all of them will be dead."* Can we take a cue from his reflection that all of mankind now living, unwilling or unable to cope with the most serious problems, will be gone, and that the world may be acquiring new generations with missions mature enough to cope with the inheritance of a world run amuck?

Whatever generations undertake to meet the problem, they must not presume to offer the continued ineffective answers we have had based on the overwhelming avarice and ecological disregard by past industrial *"authority"*.

Clearly we need to do something right now about salvaging our yet livable world. However, the reversal possibility in the face of ignorance, greed, and sex encyclicals is very questionable. The time schedule is rapidly closing in. The long-term program suggested to correct pollution could be too late.

We might for a moment reflect on the following: If, by some cataclysmic nuclear disaster, all human life were destroyed, the processes of nature would in time of their own accord clean up the earth. Rivers now fetid sewers would run crystal clear again, the smog-born air would become fresh, vegetation would refresh the earth. Why then have we not, and why do we not allow this powerful ally—Nature—to work for us now? It is always working , of course, but man's ravage exceeds it, and by this excess, ravage destroys whatever correcting processes that might operate in nature.

A first move in the right direction does, after all, show some signs of a start, in that every person capable of serious thought now appears to be recognizing that something has to be done immediately. The preliminary thinking about it is no longer adequate; we need every practical means that will spur us into physical, not rhetorical, instant action. The choking cough is becoming more convincing than the critically spoken word.

Yet, it would be rather frustrating if we succeeded in accomplishing our ecological balance to make the world physically tenable without a revaluation of individual importance. Enough has been said in previous columns to emphasize that man has been losing much of his position as an assertive, creative, and choosing individual. In the Humanistic Revolution, therefore, I am thinking of a course ahead where our attitude or way of life is centered on individual human interests and values, where the dignity, worth and self-realization of man can be achieved through reason and common decency, where regimentation and dogma cannot possibly be allowed any longer to set the general pattern of civilization.

Imbalance between birth control and the using up of our resources adds another factor of risk to an untenable future existence. When we speak of conserving our resources in proportion to our population, it means that we have the need for not only conserving our resourses to last; they must be so used as not to devastate the natural environment in the process of their current utilization. Uninhibited expansion of industry is unthinkable. Uninhibited reproduction of population is reckless world-destroying fecundity.

Most scientists agree that none of these regenerative processes can succeed unless the main focus of public action is directed immediately on contraception. No satisfactory estimate can be made of the unwanted births in the world, though I am sure that the number would be staggering. Never before has there been so great a hope in saving a rapidly deteriorating world as that which lies in the discovery of modern contraceptives. If we can repeal the legislation which prohibits their free distribution and discourage the bigotry which prevents their use, we may possibly be on our way to some practical ecological salvage of our environment.

Like all progressive change, any newly-instituted process is bound to be laboriously uphill. Conservative, materialistic minds, living in a kind of status quo smugness, attach great value to procrastination in corrective measures, using the subterfuge that inordinate delay brings a better final result. Most often it brings none, and too often it brings decay. Procrastination rests on fear or avarice for the untaxed dollar and is the common devious device used to frustrate the responsibility of national change.

Rising generations will likely enjoy the advantage of a more reciprocal viewpoint as a way of life than has existed in the past. The old desire to dominate will never die, but it will have too much rational opposition in the future for its own comfort, and any undue exercise of it is likely to meet ridicule more severe than even the arrogant dare face.

One tends in the later years of life to look back rather than forward. But in the turn of events, as I hear the shouting of student crowds outside the university and industrial walls, asking for curricular, environmental, and social change; as congregations demand repeal of sex encyclicals and suppression of dogmatic bigotry; as popery is compelled to defer to the will of enlightened congregations; as the negro and other minority groups have come to demand decency instead of pleading for it; as the student, the hippy, and kindred groups earnestly seek something from life beyond the industrial treadmill; as scientists talk of desalting seawater and purifying our once fresh bodies of water; as political parties find that their platitudes are met with ridicule and constituent rejection—on all these premises and greater promises, I have a strong feeling that whatever life remains for me, I shall look forward to it with renewed zeal and hope for man's future.

Credo: Do not live so that you *"know the price of everything and the value of nothing,"* for therein lies eventual frustration.

Nature Indispensable

There was a time, not so long ago in the early development of the country, when the majority considered the wilds in general an unrelated, distinct entity from urban or conventional life. When leaving the city, it was usually for a brief vacation to *"fish our fool heads off,"* or lie about in the sun to get the ephemeral tan. Industry talked chiefly about conquering the wilderness, and as enemy, proceeded to ravage it.

We who move gregariously in the anthill of the city must realize that we are after all, an integral, ecological part of the remote natural environment, and that unless we preserve it, we all die.

For example: The green leaf that by photosynthesis supplies the oxygen indispensable to our bodies if we are to survive, is now realized to have always been projected from the natural world into our urban life. We learned this early in school, but shunned it as of no significance in a city-obsessed life.

We need to recognize, in order to understand the viability of our place in nature, that intrinsically we are animals; noble animals on occasion to be sure, but nevertheless all of us are part of the world's fauna, and inescapably dependent upon nature.

This should not be considered a disparaging realization. Where, for example, in the whole scope of human activity, can we surpass in wonder the biological miracle?

Vigorous exercise in the uncontaminated air of the natural environment would for all, despite wilderness-living incompetence, give them a much better physical constitution, and a better intellectual insight on their own particular motives.

Few long-urban-resident people have enjoyed a truly euphoric feeling of health. By the most realistic, clinical consideration, urban life is, at best, only a maladjustment to an unnatural, air-polluted environment, a much modulated condition not realized until some radical transition inadvertently or otherwise, has been made in their lives to a natural environment, where its effect is subsequently discovered.

What needs to be emphasized is that a psychological change also becomes a big part of the transition from city to natural environment. Undeniably a cultural approach to human values does not prosper as well where there is a *"Tintinnabulation of the bells,"* screaming sirens, confusion of traffic, air pollution and severe human tensions.

There is also, no less, a matter of the aesthetic. I concede that an architectural masterpiece pleases my senses, but most temples of nature grab me more intensely in aesthetic and inspiring form than anything man has yet erected.

A strong affinity for nature has had much to do with my aversion to conventional impermanence, quite often an abhorance to early obsolescence. But perhaps the factor which lies most deeply-seated is the lack of fulfillment commonly believed to lie in the acquisition of material things. Even the acquisition-dollars-for-affluence fades miserably in the prospect of an interest in nature and profound cultural values.

Thoreau said about the excessive pursuit of industrial wealth, *"They will find it a fool's life when they get to the end of it if not before."*

Time, obviously, is the greatest poverty of all with each of us.

John Muir discovered wilderness and became an immortal by his depiction of it in the eyes of at least the comprehensive-minded world. His father, on the other hand, said, *"Wilderness is a sinful waste,"* myoptically his eye was confined to the plow and dogma.

It is obvious that the population of our country which has gone to the suburbs to outer suburbia and beyond, where they can pursue profound cultural values in a natural environment will have come closer to life's fulfillment in whatever basic pursuits they have, than most who are caught in the urban bondage.

Some people can get used to living next door to an abattoir. If I have a choice, I prefer not to be their neighbors.

Credo: Since we are mammalian, nature is indispensable to our existence.

Walden

The most salient reason why a current column should be written about a book published a hundred or more years ago, is that its pertinence applies significantly and even more poignantly today than it did when published.

"*Walden*", written by David Henry Thoreau scarcely aroused the attention of his local peers in Concord, Massachusetts. Today it has spread round the world in various translations. I call attention to its publication on tape, it being a best seller among those driving the busy traffic lanes.

What essentially is it all about? Let Thoreau tell you in his own words:

"*When I wrote the following pages, or rather the bulk of them, I lived alone, in the woods, a mile from any neighbor, in a house which I had built myself, on the shore of Walden Pond, in Concord, Massachusetts, and earned my living by the labor of my hands only. I lived there two years and two months. At present I am a sojourner in civilized life again.*"

It was here in a tiny cabin that Thoreau made the observations that, figuratively speaking, have been "*shots heard round the world.*"

He advised that, "*It would be to some advantage to live a primitive and frontier life, though in the midst of an outward civilization, if only to learn what are the gross necessisities of life and what methods (and I add, time) have been taken to obtain them . . .*"

Thoreau, a champion against the glut of materialism and social conformity, has had his vindictive critics. Where intellectual competence among his students is concerned, he has been and is becoming a philosophical and literary discovery. Those who are bent on derision, find themselves befuddled by the fact that in "*Walden*" there is no vulnerable statistical data to attack. Thoreau made no attempt to depict life's potentials digitally. His euphemisms, subtle humor, apothegms, keen insight on human motives, satire, his exposure of conventional idolatry, and the rest, have been too abstractly elusive in substance to be tracked down by critics whose life's values are measured largely by the scale of gross national products.

Thoreau's hope for a civilization capable of comprehending and enjoying a more natural world, is what troubles a press being bought up through merger to favor ravage of natural resources for excessive pecuniary profit at the expense of a viable world.

Those critics who deride Thoreau are obviously indigent of any truly significant natural life experience. The problem is that they have apparently only a blushing acquaintance with the wilds and yet presume (in silent desperation, of course) to be imbued with its profound nature. So they presumptuously say, *"I like the wilderness but. . ."* Which connotes that they are alien to it in all except perhaps an occasional fleeting glance.

Thus we have a share of professorial English literature pedants hoping to reduce the insurmountable magnitude of *"Walden"* into brief derogatory essays. At best they become pusillanimous and inept. Inept because I know of none among them who, through their writing, have manifested a sufficiently Thoreauan-like wilderness experience. Having spent about half of each year in the wilds in all seasons, and written a dozen books on the subject, I can speak with at least some advisability of their critique.

Failing to penetrate to any depth the inscrutable wilderness, the derogatory critics have hoped to label *"Walden"* an overture into transcendentalism. This is the old trick of indulging their incompetence in the hocus pocus of trying to keep their readers believing that what they offer is profound, when in reality it is largely obscurantism—opposition to honest enlightenment.

Transcendentalism: *"The belief that knowledge of reality is derived from intuitive sources rather than from objective experience,"* is a definition that resolves itself into semantic humbug. One must presume from this Kantian, transcendentalist nonsense that if one stubbed and broke the bones in a toe, it actually didn't happen but was simply an intuitive caprice of the victim.

So we can presume from the derogatory critics that when Thoreau studiously and pleasurably roamed the hills around Concord, probed the inner sanctum of the wilderness for his material, and otherwise engaged in the study of world-wide subjects, expressed in his writings, these had no basis in reality but were mere intuitive notions of actuality.

Thoreau's humor also escapes the too-utilitarian mind. He says, *"I am an inspector of snowstorms."* This *"bugs"* his critics.

His essay on Civil Disobedience has been a great chapter in the world's judiciary.

His influence upon those who have sought a more natural life has been tremendous. *"In wilderness,"* he says, *"is the preservation of the world."*

We can presume that his influence upon individualism might eventually become one of the greatest forces against popular conformism—the herd mind.

We have come to a period in the world community when Thoreau's plea for simplicity of living (thus more artful and viable) will not be just one of a needed culture, but the direction we can take in the saving of the world from materialistic catastrophe.

He suggested that we so live in artful simplicity that we can do our bookkeeping on our thumbnail. This euphemism also *"bugs"* his critics.

Credo: If you have not read *"Walden"*, do so for the cultivation of life; for a road of escape from the mass mind; from a tyrannizing materialism; and for a freshening of the spirit.

You Don't Steer A Horse

Peter, age 8, answered the phone last night when I called his father. Before I could make my request, Peter spoke up, *"You want to talk to my father?"*

"First," I said, *"I'd like to talk to you."* (Kids are so frequently shunted aside.)

Peter told me that he had been given a pinto pony, that he didn't ride him much in winter because the weather was so cold. *"I can't wear my mittens,"* he said, *"because if I do, I can't steer, and my feet get cold from the iron pedals."*

Well, there you have modern youth, so imbued with mechanized nomenclature that the pinto pony got to be a robot.

"Peter," I said, *"you don't steer a horse, you guide or rein him, and your feet go into stirrups, not on pedals."*

His father, highly amused, then in turn asked Peter if he thought spurs were accelerators.

A university professor, acting as coordinator on a TV show, failed a contestant when he used the word 'hames'. *"There's no such word,"* said the professor.

To his dismay he found there was (a part of the collar assembly of a horse's harness), and the contestant had to be brought back. He also learned that a crupper was that part of a harness that goes under the horse's tail. If I were a horse, and they put a crupper under my tail, I think I'd take to bucking.

Learning about Peter's mechanically-motivated pinto pony, I recalled what Walter McFarlane, one of Canada's highly successful wilderness artists told me.

"Do you realize," he said, *"that few people have known the wilderness without planes, outboard motors, chain saws, ice hole augers, snowmobiles, trail bikes, radios, radio telephones, and other such contrivances?"* Adding, *"And how superior the wilds were without them."*

Winston Churchill said that the invention of the internal combustion engine was the greatest curse ever imposed on mankind. Could he have foreseen the oil shortage?

Perhaps we will discover that in thirty years (the predicted end of the world's oil supply), we might get back to much healthful manual effort. The earth's resources are finite—not an idle fact of speculation but now a basic concept given a great deal of scientific consideration in long-time industrial planning.

In a storm or other emergency when electrical power gets cut off, refrigeration stops, gas and oil furnaces quit, water taps do not yield water, lights go out; in short, our lives are suddenly turned back a century or more to simple elemental living.

Yet, I found that most people respond to this quite admirably. A warmth of neighborliness and cooperation ensues. A few people gripe but they usually are the ones who gripe under the best of conditions.

When my wife, Florence, and I head into the Canadian wilds, and are on the canoe routes or winter trails, we of course have to forego the button-pressing conveniences. Yet, we eat good meals cooked over wood fires, sleep comfortably and warm in down robes on air mattresses, missing nothing really except the turbulance of a moderated urban life—something we forego readily to an advantage.

Thoreau in his book WALDEN, suggested that we try living in the simple cabin for a while, to learn how dispensable most of what we strive to acquire actually is.

Most of us in one way or another become addicted to modern mechanization. We might, in one sense, regard this as sound expedience if it were tempered somewhat. When my wife and I, for example, encounter the fast rivers and head winds of big water in Canada's wilderness, we are glad to have an outboard motor. But there are calm days when the lakes are placid; most segments of rivers flow gently. Life then calls for serenity and contemplation. To use an outboard motor on such days would be to lose the natural values of the wilds. In the same sense, those persons in cities who use their cars to travel a mere two or three blocks have little utility sense as to the value of motor transportation.

Perhaps the value of modernization can be summed up in a sentence or two. If we devote our entire lives to acquiring it, how much time has it saved us? If we do not soon get leisure with security by building up the big pile, what have we gained?

Credo: Let's not overlook the miracle of our manual capability.

Wilderness Enow

I quote the following abstracts from my book, *"Once Upon A Wilderness"*, chapter 17, The *"Wilderness Tomorrow"*, (Macmillan N.Y., N.Y.).

"Let's suppose for a moment that in the United States with its onrushing population increases, there is still a wilderness area of nearly a million acres that has been left just about as wild and untrammeled as it was a thousand years ago. In the play of our imagination, let's consider that only the rare individual has ever visited this grand expanse of nature."

"Incredible even to the imagination? It seems so today. It's like the fellow who said, 'Imagine it: a thick steak, salad, baked potato, beverage and dessert all for thirty-five cents'. A bystander asked, 'Where can I get this meal for thirty-five cents?' The reply, 'I don't know, but just imagine it!'"

"Should we be as facetiously speculative about the dream-wilderness described?"

"We don't have to imagine it. It actually does exist. Every phase described is factual on Unimak Island, only a part of the wilderness region in the Alaskan conservation proposal."

Dec. One, '78, President Carter signed the proposal to set aside a substantial part of the Alaskan wilds, where no mining, forestry or hunting will be permitted.

It is as hard to believe as the thirty-five-cent steak dinner. If President Carter ultimately fails to bring about peace in the Israel-Egypt conflict, if he loses a correction handle on the nefarious inflation greed scandal, if his civil-rights, human decency program fails influence, I shall nevertheless with gusto in my writing program henceforth proclaim him a big cut above the many stereotype presidents whose records are in the dusty archives.

My hat is also off to the National Congress who saved our Boundary Waters Canoe Area from provincial profiteers, those who would be glad to destroy whatever is invaluable in order to add a sovereign to their glut.

Central Park in New York City came under pressure awhile ago as being a waste of land. It was needed, we were told, for the profit it would bring as high-rise sites. Has moronism become virtuous?

What staggers the imagination of anybody who has enough sense to pack sand in a rat hole, is why do people who have the opportunity of position accede to the picayune, to the provincialism of the greedy, to anything and anybody who can skim off some excess profit or votes?

If they were cognizant of history they would see that their politically picayunish approach to life, their surrender to both plebeian and corporate greed, makes them as dispensable as yesterday's garbage.

How avidly people seek office! We can presume that it is a hope of being in the limelight. But how few have the nobility of mind to seek values once they are elected. For every one who rises above mediocrity there are thousands who are lost in limbo, soon forgotten entities who should not in the first place because of their incompetence and questionable integrity have been elected to office. Many I found in my earlier days as an investigator of crime on a national basis, sought office so that they could nefariously play into the hands of an element who subsidized their campaigns.

In the preservation of our wilderness areas from ravage we need to keep aware of the fact that while we have gained some advantage in conserving some of our natural resources, eternal vigilance will be necessary to keep the ravagers from destroying the last vestage of natural values.

One of the most encouraging aspects of late has been that industry in a few anomalous cases is boasting at considerable advertising cost, that they are projecting their expansion without the usual devastating destruction of natural values. It might catch on. The late mode of advertising has been to unscrupulously name and condemn the competitive product. If the creditable minority of industry will now likewise name and expose the ravagers, progress could make a sudden transition. At least it might keep out of our crowded courts the ravagers who bring in a whole mob of attorneys to overwhelm the judiciary for the right to destroy our natural resources for excessive profits.

There is no more commendable profession in our social complex than the practice of law when the attorney seeks to prevent the imposition of tyranny. But when lawyers defer to the infamous, to those who become desperate to destroy our natural values for excessive profit, then infamy has reached a new low. There is no judicial or rational denial here that everybody is entitled to a trial and defense. But here we have an unscrupulous element hoping that they will have the right to continue destroying human values for pecuniary profit, and apparently would over-ride judiciary, human decency or any other obstruction to satisfy their infamous greed.

Credo: It is believed by some able scientists that man is the endangered species. We need to prevent those in authority from killing off all of us. They seem wanting to pave the earth for pecuniary greed.

Remembered or Forgotten Senators

Senators Gaylord Nelson (D-Wis.), John Durkin (D-N.H.), and Gary Hart (D-Colo.), who so admirably have sought to preserve the 110 million acres of Alaskan natural lands and other potential areas, are names to remember—names that very likely will be carried over into posterity.

We might stop to ask why the expression of these particular senators should paradoxically stand out as a news feature. Where, we ask, are the other senators who can be presumed to have a sense for natural values?

We can hope that a few of them are not contained in that long list of genuflectors to industry—a list great enough down through history to paper the walls of our national and state capitols with documented failures.

They wonder why they become forgotten entities. They loom up momentarily for a term of office like a photoflashbulb, and as ephemerally go into discard.

Their shrift being short, the answer as to why becomes obvious. They are too provincially limited in legislative compass, naturalistic understanding, and what constitutes nobility of action. As senators they are not concerned with the broad senatorial responsibility attributed to them, but tend to be what we might term aldermanic in scope. They are, in short, hog-tied to some greedy provincial lust in their own home bailiwick, or some industry.

We saw this in the B.W.C.A. political fracas. Preservation of a great national monument became politically involved in a fish-glut syndrome for the local fisherman and fishing camp industry. who wanted to invade the canoe country lakes and fish them to death, as they have the far more numerous other lakes, outside of the B.W.C.A.

This low-mentality fishing from daylight to dark; what is it, a psychopathic offshoot from the dollar-grubbing syndrome where most cultural values are preempted? The sadistic desire to feel a fish struggling for its life must surely be a form of narcotism. It is called *"a fight"*. The opponent? Should not one hook at the other end of the line be in a swimming fisherman's mouth to make the whole contest come up to Queensbury rules?

Have I strayed from my subject of politicians? Not at all. It was a deference by senatorial candidates largely to this fishing syndrome, rather than to the importance of a national monument that had the senatorial candidates in a dither during the Minnesota election of 1978.

What, actually, is basic in all this?

Essentially it comes down to a matter of one element wanting to ravage every available area for profit, while another element tries to understand values and wants to preserve them in order to make life tenable generally.

Make no mistake about it. We have a vast horde, both industrial and plebeian, who would ravage the earth to extinction for pecuniary profit if they could get away with it.

We can make exception only to that small amount of creditable industry and the lay population who are trying to maintain some degree of environmental viability.

The media recently reported that approximately 800 distinct areas in the United States are now in serious jeopardy from hazardous chemical dumps alone. All water in varying degrees is polluted. Industry is perpetually in courts to continue this ravage by legal decree.

Make up your mind as to the integrity then of those politicians who are on the side of industry fighting for the right to continue this pollution wherever it can contribute to excessive profits. Recently industry succeeded in getting the E.P.A. to lower the pollution standard. Human health and a viable environment have become more expendable than excess profits.

Here in the reckless process of industrial ravage of the environment is where the money is; and here in the consequent stench is where suspect politicians are buzzing like blow flies on carrion.

Consider, on the other hand, the politicians who seek to resolve problems and try to become statesmen. Consider again the disadvantage that they have in emerging on the strength of their own credibility and a sane viable program. Then ponder the fact that down through history only a few have emerged to be celebrated. It takes a lot of courage and honesty.

When the Gaylord Nelsons, the Durkins, Harts, Udalls and those like them refuse to be pawns and seek to save the higher values of human existence, do not simply take them for granted, for such as they, are the beneficial kingdom of the earth. Salute them, and by your vote keep them in office, for they hold the bastion that keeps us from totally losing our sense of values.

The Alaska Lands' Issue has been called *"The most important environmental decision that will be made in our generation."*

Unless we exercise the most profound wisdom, we soon won't have to make that decision at all. The advocates of free industrial ravage will turn our magnificent world into the garbage of desolation. They will have paved the most priceless natural areas with ribbons of asphalt, reduced the air to lung-carcinogen potentials, water to septic reservoirs, land to chemical hazard, and the human race to another endangered species. Though we finally could become a nation of morons stumbling around waiting to die off, there will be one great asset: we will have turned everything worth selling into cash and have the whole net proceeds of human aspiration on earth deposited in the bank. For once, money would indisputably be everything—in value, nothing.

That seems the trend of how we have been plunging ahead.

Change for the better generally comes when we have reached the saturation point and get only diminishing returns, but if we go too far with our industrial desolation, restoration may be too expensive, too intractable, too far on the back road to return.

We need to take into consideration that we have along with a strong minimal conservation force in Washington, also a horde of disparagers cowering at the feet of industry, whom we are supporting at high salaries. Could it be that eventually we will have enough enlightenment to track down the despoilers and get rid of at least the worst ones in our succeeding elections?

Credo: We can earnestly hope that fools are not in the majority, for then in any plebiscite we will have the low-caste politician to contend with; where human values are subordinate to political nefariousness.

Under Water

"Woe unto the man who builds his house upon the sand." And woe unto the family that build their house upon the flood plain.

The big snows of 1978-79 again had houses flooded to the second story, garages, when not properly anchored, floating downstream.

Nature on a rampage? Not really. A matter obviously, more of residential maladjustment. Nature is not an obedient respector of persons. As the spring floods come from spring to spring, and from flash rains to flash rains, as they have eternally, the government is blamed for not building dikes, failure to give evacuation warnings; in fact, irrationally blamed for nature's variable processes.

I am tempted at such times to take the position of a man who saw a snake digesting the leg of a frog, the body of which was too big to swallow. *"How cruel,"* I commented. The man looking on said, *"My sentiments are with the snake."* It was nature; why fight it or fear its ugliness.

As floods recede, no lesson is learned. The flood will, no doubt, be repeated. No effort will be made to move to higher ground or accept the floods with insurance to compensate for the loss.

One family I know loads items of floodable damage into a moving van, stores the items until after recession of the flood, hires a cleanup and decorating crew, and moves back until the next flood threat; a mere routine.

This is expensive, of course, and might seem a nuisance, but I know the family and it is one that accepts life on its own terms. There is no griping, no protest to the government. They want to live down on the riverfront, and for that they are willing to meet whatever it entails. Not every year, of course, does the river reach the high flood mark, but when it threatens they are ready.

What the reader will observe here is that the adversities of life are met by this family as a resolvable process, not considered a calamity. It is a philosophic approach which can, figuratively speaking, be applied to many of our woes as method. As one said, *"I seek solutions."*

The instability of nature has been a challenge to mankind since his inception. I have written several books on how one should meet the weather adversities in wilderness areas. Fair-weather campers as wilderness travelers are always in trouble when nature's mood changes.

On a canoe trip in Canada my partner and I traveled on a smooth stretch of river with low-lying banks that beckoned the pitching of a tent. Once in camp we remarked, *"Wouldn't this be an ideal place for a cabin?"*

At two a.m. when we were about half-way through a calm night of sleep, the moon gibbous, the sky star-studded, no sign of rain, we awoke to find our mattresses awash. That beautifully lying camp area was under water. Somewhere a long way back upriver over the horizon a cloudburst had obviously dropped a heavy rain. It could have been a half day or longer before it reached us.

Soon our canoe lying upside down nearby would have been afloat, headed downriver, had we not been awakened by our watery bed. All of our gear, including provisions were in waterproof bags so that no loss was incurred.

High land was a hundred feet or more back from where our tent stood pitched in water. The moon and stars lighted our way as we decamped and portaged to the higher ground.

Aroused by physical activity, we made no effort to re-camp but built a drying out fire, prepared breakfast and watched the first rays of dawn stealing over the Northland. As we traveled on we were just behind a wall of water that traveled ahead of us. Since that experience we have sought higher camp areas, even though more attractive ones lay nearer to the water's edge.

In New Mexico an irrigation dam was built on the Pecos River, the river expected to create a reservoir with the accumulation of water over several years. An historical five days of rain in the mountains filled the reservoir, nearly taking out the dam by the impact of the rushing, high wall of water.

Arroyos sometimes get such rushing walls of water. Where roads cross the arroyos, cars have been caught at the impending time-coincidence of such walls of water, sending the cars rolling over and over, crushed and killing the occupants.

One learns the power of rushing water when running rapids and the waves of windblown, large lakes with a canoe, or other craft.

On the other hand, there are the days of placid water on wilderness lakes, and stretches of river that flow with the smoothness of mercury.

To glide along on such days in a canoe and contemplate the scene, gives us the feeling that there is a great deal more benevolence in water than fury, and, as we can presume there is more kindness in humanity than ill will. When water runs rampant and ill will is provoked, we might consider as did our philosophic resident on the flood plain: both might be resolved with method and wisdom.

Credo: We can afford to resolve problems—not fight them.

Eminent Domain

The power line dispute in Western Minnesota and elsewhere is a dilemma that harks back by eminent domain to the early development of the country.

When land was cheap and much of it was still owned by the government, few problems arose in declaring rights-of-way for vehicle-roads, railroads, and power lines. These essentials to the welfare of settlement were looked upon as great blessings. Today, we take them for granted. True, there were some provincial conflicts earlier between the stagecoach, railroads, and horse-trucking freight routes—even with some land owners. But these were of minimal infringement in a new, wide-open country, and did not overall become very significant.

What seemed to be a necessary and integral part of a developing nation, inadvertently gave industry carte blanche; that is, unrestricted power to act at its own discretion. It hasn't, unfortunately, had the discretionary capability to handle this. It became heavy-handed.

What has created the big problem is that some irresponsible industry believes that in its condoned right to move freely, it has a prerogative to run rough-shod whenever and wherever it chooses over the rights of individuals in their privacy of ownership.

When industry has run up against the sovereign rights of the individual, instead of considering that right over and beyond the strict letter of the law, it frequently overwhelms the courts, knowing that the individual can't cost-wise meet the opposition, where dollar equity dominates the judiciary in their thinking.

By law we are, of course, required to condone this. What we can't legally, or otherwise condone, what history has shown, is that much industry—and even on occasion the unions have had the audacity to set the cultural pattern of the Nation, something far out of their intellectual province. Everything gets reduced to industrial profit, seldom to a cultural, humane and rational resolution; always price, seldom value.

When it gets to abridgement of the individual's sovereign rights, such as running a power line rough-shod over a farmer's private domain, neither industry, farmer, nor government knows what the hell to do about it. Good sense is replaced with boorish judiciary. Frustrated farmers resort to vandalism.

There is on this same theme, an effort in force now to consolidate newspapers and perhaps book publishing companies into one vast cartel. This, if it succeeds, will eventually eliminate all individual points of view and rights. When the eminent domain whip is cracked, we as individuals, had better jump, or the government that keeps us under the eminent domain thumb will rush in as it has in the power line dispute—soldiers dragging us bodily, sacrosanctly, culturally and sentimentally off of our own property and away from our own ideas in favor of industrial eminent domain.

The state legislature could get busy and make some provision for an accepted construction method for power lines, but if there is anyone over there in the legislature with any creative sense, it hasn't been manifest in several basic industrial problems that have dogged us in recent years.

The reckless pollution of Lake Superior got to be not a natural resource pollution problem, but another legal battle in which industry swarmed the court with opposing legal talent. Neither industry, its legal talent, nor the state gave any serious heed to a satisfactory, natural-resource solution.

The resolution got to be one of half measures where exorbitant industrial profit won over a weak commonwealth, a weaker legislature and governor. A valid solution was possible, just as there is a valid solution to the power line dispute, but we do not have enough astutely credible people to resolve it.

These aspirants to political and industrial positions—their eye myoptically on the dollar—are incapable of conducting their political or industrial office any higher than a passable, obtuse mediocrity. They merely get by. Yet, each in his own egocentricity sees himself rising prodigiously into higher office.

As to their achievement? We usually can write their biographies forty years in advance, barring accidents.

Credo: Magnanimity requires an intellectually generous mind.

The Firearms Dilemma

Whenever an attempt is made to register firearms, two obstacles get into the way, the N.R.A. (National Rifle Association) and the Constitution—a not too well defined permission of the citizen's right to bear arms. Both obstacles are more imposing than at first we might presume.

The love of firearms is understandable. As one who has traveled by canoe and dogsled in the North American wilderness through much of my life, I saw the necessity to carry arms for survival. Not protection against wild animals, I hasten to add, but for living off the country when the carrying of store provision for months of travel would have been prohibitive in weight.

I can say that the need of firearms in the wilds for protection is largely an illusion. Wolves do not surround campfires where flaming fagots have to be thrown at them to deter their onslaughts upon the campers as fiction has told us. One may live in a country well populated with wolves and never see one, so elusive are they. Bears keep their distance from people but one might have a rifle handy only for comfort if one has a fear of bears. Where camp provisions are left unguarded, even for short periods, bears can be a nuisance, and may have to be shot.

A man, wife and an 8 year old son out on a hike in the Alaska wilds found their son running up a knoll highly interested in something. When the parents reached the top of the knoll they saw a grizzly bear in rapid retreat from the sight of their 8 year old.

At one time I was highly interested in guns. I had so much involvement in them I could give the ballistics of nearly every cartridge in the world offhand. Guns were displayed in a rack in the most conspicuous part of my household. I polished the stocks, oiled and worked the actions, and had flights of fancy as to their killing power. I planned their complement in every detail for the long wilderness journeys which I took annually.

But in my whole lifetime I have not hunted for sport. I never killed for fun something that dearly wanted to live. Even when I had the need for shooting part of my food on the long wilderness journey, I killed with great reluctance. In later years I doubled and tripled the carries over portages with extra food packs in order to avoid killing wildlife for food. Later when I could get planes to deliver store food packs to me at some portage or camp several hundred miles back in the wilds, at a specific time of rendezvous, I left the firearms behind, happily relieved of their care and weight.

I still have the firearms I used in those days, not conspicuously displayed in a rack, but cleaned, oiled and packed away in chests, where I seldom look at them.

I have no rapport with hunters who *"kill for fun"*.

It is psychotic to say that the father and son who slay together, stay together. I can understand the hunter's love of firearms but I find fault with the purpose to which he adapts them—the joy of slaughter. In a finite world of endangered wildlife species, I find the hunter on a tragically low intellectual level when he seeks to reduce the wildlife population just to satisfy his killing syndrome.

In an aggregate sense, he seems to have little love of the wild. He rushes out for the kill and its legal limit, and on acquiring it, as quickly rushes back to his urban life, surely a pusillanimous venture.

A lecturer from Australia visiting the United States filled an auditorium with hunters and fishermen, and in testing his audience with twenty average natural history and outdoor-life questions listed on a card to be filled out during intermission, he found that out of a possible one hundred score, the average of his audience was about twenty-two.

In sudden blizzards during hunting season, hunters died in substantial numbers from a lack of basic survival knowledge. Theirs is the full bag limit, and to that they avariciously struggle.

The contribution of hunting license fees to propagation is considerable, but the boast here can be only that propagation is for continued slaughter, not preservation.

The theory that hunting maintains a mammalian ecological balance is false, since hunters kill healthy animals, where predators consume weak and old animals.

The falling off of game bag limits set by law, makes evident that we are losing our propagation efforts in most species. The matter of registering firearms has become a national political battle. There are good arguments on both sides of this issue.

It may seem a bit absurd to think that a successful invasion of the United States by a totalitarian army would be easier if it were known who of the citizens had arms. I nevertheless feel more comfortable in knowing that if such an invasion were attempted, every household in a sense would be found an arsenal.

On the other hand, I hark back to my earlier life when I was employed on a national basis as an investigator of crime. Had we known then who owned certain firearms, so that we could have made identifying ballistic checks of slugs and primers, our job would have been greatly facilitated.

To have all this ballistics identification data at one's finger-tips from a computer, would be to so cramp the style of hoodlums, police and judicial systems would finally have the upper hand.

Those legally in possession of firearms would likely get them back if stolen, through this computer method.

Credo: Our greatest safety may be in the domestically hidden arsenal. But I would feel better about the hunter if he put a love of the wilds far above his love of slaughter.

The Abortion Dilemma

There will, no doubt, always remain a few dilemmas in human life—predicaments that seemingly defy solutions. Perhaps we need them to keep us vitally conscious of our existential place in society and the natural world.

Since both prohibition and the legalized sale of alcoholic liquors have been proven failures, if we observe the extent of alcoholism, we can regard this as one of the major dilemmas. What runs it a close second, if not first, is birth control, and all its underlying precepts: planned parenthood, general contraception and abortion. The public being evenly divided on this issue, the controversy promises to go into perpetuity. All but abortion in the birth control argument are, however, fairly well resolved, although much residual confusion on the overall contraceptive problem still exists.

Early in February 1978, the National Broadcasting Company reported that the world population, by various effects is decreasing in number. Contraception, abortion, greatly increased cost of education beyond the average budget, inflation, sterilization of both male and female—all these seem to have entered into population reduction. We might, it seems, by this world news, at least avoid being ultimately buried in our own refuse.

The concept of *standing room only* on the earth has now become just one of those old-wives-tales. There has, nevertheless, existed a valid belief that the population would geometrically increase to over-populate the earth. Approximately four billion people are alive on the earth today. But we overlook the fact that in the span of about one hundred years, every one of us now existing will have vanished. Somewhere contained in the elements of the earth, the air and the sun are the molecular potentials of another four billion people to replace us.

The human body is largely water, and a very small amount of molecular solids. Those elements lie in the earth now—an inspiring potential—waiting to be vivified into human and numerous other creatures; and, of course, the emergence, too, of the recycling flora.

What gives abortion its intangible twist is that none of us will ever be able to pin down its earliest stages when by abortion a *viable, full statutory* life is eliminated. The clinical and legal world is as much in a dilemma on this score as the layman.

What gets us all so hopelessly involved in the complexity of the abortion problem is that we have not been able to draw a sharp distinction between the life-destroying potential of contraception and abortion. When contraceptive methods are used, the plan, of course, is to destroy the potential of human life. Therefore, any contraception procedure we indulge ourselves in outside of having offspring as consecutively as biologically possible—say about twenty or more babies to a couple (heaven forbid!)—becomes a factual matter of destroying the potentials of human life in all except those who were actually given birth—fortunately, not twenty.

From the time conception occurs to the moment of birth, we have to consider if this life-potential of sperm and ovum is different in destructive liability from the potential of destroying the fetus itself, as a life potential. Most will say, though wrongly, that contraception is *not* destroying life, although in truth, it is.

The problem then becomes current as to whether abortion surgery can come under *Medicare.* The position taken on this phase by the anti-abortionists is apparently the hope that by shutting off *Medicare* assistance they can avoid the cost of abortion being incurred by the public treasury. The best estimate is that where the poor are concerned, the resulting cost of having unwanted children born and supported by the state would be a drain on the public treasury, perhaps five to ten times the cost of that which would be dispersed from *Medicare*-allowed abortions.

Where abortion becomes illegal, or too restricted, the bootlegger *"clinician"* moves in en masse. This incurs serious ramifications of misery, even greater than what the prohibition-day bootlegger caused.

I have been told hearsay, and found it not denied clinically, that there is now a low-risk, do-it-yourself abortion kit being developed, which, if true, will likely place the responsibility wholly on the pregnant individual.

Law, of course, will eventually have to draw the demarcation line, if it ever can, between life-emergence of the sperm-ovum combination, and the fetus. I am sure it cannot.

On the concluding list of resolutions, should be a decision based on amniocentesis, the process of determining before birth, whether a fetus will be born a viable being. Opponents here, we hope, might find merciful agreement on abortion.

However we manage to resolve this problem, if ever, we need to consider that abortions will continue, by women going to states or countries where abortion is legal—states or countries that will, no doubt, reap vast clinical and ambient revenue as a result. This can become so pecuniarily competitive that few states eventually will be able to afford maintaining legislation against publicly subsidized abortion.

Credo: Don't make women incubators of the state against their will.

The Juvenile Gap

The human fetus—if it escapes demise by abortion—occupies the most accommodating environment of its prospective life.

Being born becomes its first ordeal. The loud protest it makes upon the culmination of birth, is evidence of the distressing transition it has just made.

Once settled into its crib it will do a lot of sleeping, but when awake, it will demand—usually with howling success—food and assurance of its security.

The warm hand of the nurse stroking its back is consolation enough that it has not been abandoned.

In a hospital nursery I watched a nurse pick up a baby and put it through the feeding and care routine—the baby wailing violently from momentary neglect. The nurse unaffected emotionally, remarked *"It thinks the world owes it a living."*

Certainly the world owes that much to its helpless years, since it had no choice in its inception.

Just when responsibility should become a part in the child's training will remain moot.

Wilderness Indian babies confined to their tikinakuns (cradle boards) are left hanging in trees for hours.

When they emerge from this man-made cocoon and begin to walk, they first experience the perception of touch (tactility) by being in crawling contact with the earth. Soon they learn to gather wood for campfire fuel, build cooking fires, help or in childlike fashion simulate the many parental functions of daily life; gradually with the increasing years, become responsible members of the tribe.

Obviously there is a manual sense developed here during the most impressionable years, which urban, conventional life usually does not offer.

Responsibility thus is assumed as a play routine, becoming an interestingly-acquired function of daily life.

Can it be that in city life there is a serious gap here where youth cannot fulfill a need to be part of the life it will have to assume in adulthood? And does it not place youth in a precarious position for want of something to occupy the juvenile risk years? Could this gap in the developing years be responsible for drug addiction, juvenile crime and an introduction to adult crime?

Have we thus failed to provide the means of transition from childhood to adulthood in city life? We spend billions on juvenile crime; why not spend part of that money for the transition-interest that will provide mergence from youth to adulthood. Kids like at least to simulate what adults do.

Often the demand of youth is made upon its parents with seemingly little appreciation. The presumption here apparently being that parents have had the exquisite pleasure (?) of rearing their offspring.

This, if I may be allowed a note of humor, in some instances might be akin to the fellow who purchased a pig in the fall for twenty dollars and sold it in the spring for twenty dollars. When he was told, *"You can't make any money that way,"* he replied, *"I realize that, but you see I had the use of the pig all winter,"* I suspect that some parent will consider the corollary here fitting.

In my addressing a convention audience of the American Camping Association, a number of eyebrows and some ire was raised when I suggested that we place more emphasis on individuality and less on daily regimentation of campers. I was thinking of the need for initiative and responsibility.

Later, I made an individuality-experiment with a group of youngsters which proved quite successful. This has been described at length elsewhere so will omit it in this column.

I did not consider it an imposing responsibility when in my youth I shined shoes on the city street, peddled newspapers, cleaned greasy pans in a bakery, went from house to house sharpening kitchen knives and scissors, worked as helper on delivery trucks, etcetera, etcetera.

Relief would have seemed like mooching on my fellow men. My family occasionally made full meals at dinner time from only oatmeal and milk, often enough to make hamburger now and then a memory. But we never went hungry and we never had to mooch.

I realize that the industrial and business world is so set up as to place the obligation of employment on industry and the government. But even here we cannot sit around and wait for things to happen.

We often tend to teach our youth sloth, or that they should have an allowance over and above their needs. The wise parent is one who assigns household tasks to their kids for every dollar they receive. It becomes the lesson that there are no free lunches in life, and when gifts are forthcoming, they are bonuses from the heart.

From the nursery evolve kindly people, prodigies and a share of scoundrels.

One writer lamented the fact that we did not have the predeterminative faculty of foreseeing early the birth of scoundrels, so they could be eliminated.

In amniocentesis we do have some knowledge in determining if a fetus will be born viable.

With the advent of DNA, we have come so close to having the secret of the gene, we might just possibly in time be able to steer the course of human viability.

Also we now have, for want of space, what we can call test-tube babies. This and DNA have been so frightening, a movement was started to outlaw further research into the inception of human life.

With the advent of the pill, a modification of abortion laws, and a discouraging economy, kids are growing scarce. We can't afford to waste this potential of the future world.

Credo: Perhaps we can now treasure, develop and educate our youth for enough guru responsibility to help correct the ecological and social mess we have made of our world.

Our Boomerang Conduct

A boomerang, as many know, is a flat, curved, wooden missile used by aborigines for hunting, which can be so hurled that it returns to the thrower.

The nature of the boomerang has become figurative in our speech: something we say that rebounds profitably or detrimentally. In the latter sense it suggests retaliation. The offensive remark, for instance does not remain with the person offended; it invariably boomerangs.

As we have currently seen, the result can be a lost friendship, a quarrel, a fight, a murder, a war: all losers, no gains.

A kindly remark on the other hand comes back too, but can build up to such proportions that *"crumbs thrown on the water bring back loaves"*—in short, rebounds with a kindly, elevating response.

What is often not well understood is that the offensive remark does incur retaliatory risk. It makes those we offend stronger, fiercer and more desperate. We often, as a result, pay consequent, unexpected penalties of retaliation.

For example: We heterosexuals (no doubt, in the lowest ebb of our sanity) might have believed that we struck a good blow for morality when, by local plebiscite, we were able to disenfranchise the constitutional rights of homosexuals. Not considering its boomerang effect, we believed that homosexuals knocked down would stay down. But in essence as Nietzsche said: If this does not kill them, they will be stronger. By our persecution of homosexuals, they do seem to be growing in strength as an effective force to contend with.

As much as we heterosexuals abhor the homosexual biological approach to sex, we need to recognize that homosexuals can become a formidable, retaliatory, litigation force of millions of average-to-high intelligent individuals—as a money force in the aggregate at least, people of substantial means who obviously will react through our courts, and perhaps economically. We certainly don't need enemies.

If the rumors and the proposed judicial appeals which have been bandied about are potentially correct, the boomerang could come back with a disturbing, legal and economic, costly retaliatory effect on most of us.

For example, there has been an accelerating opinion among some church denominations and the growing secular element that all church property should be currently taxed in full. Reinforcement of this opinion caused by the church's attack on homosexuals at least by their secular element, could now seriously threaten the church's position taxwise, by adversary reinforcement from the homosexual element.

The substantial sums of money being made available for litigation in getting this tax levy to the Supreme Court could thus threaten the church property free-tax status. This is amplified by the fact that taxwise, church property is already on questionable, constitutional grounds, and the church has obviously declared itself the contesting enemy of homosexuals for such taxing provocation.

Perhaps in view of this threat alone, the disenfranchised constitutional-rights-boomerang against the homosexuals should not have been thrown at them in the first place. Constitutional disenfranchisement by local plebiscite is dangerous, since it can attack any minority. As a result, we are sailing in troubled, controversial waters that may last forever—a hazard, obviously, to all, by the imposing enemy-imminence factor.

In earlier days in some countries homosexuals were indiscriminately thrown in jail. If we consider this a valid indictment, consider also that another minority element of extraordinary intelligence, keen perception, and high character were burned at the stake in the New England States, as witches. Apparently, we are still, figuratively speaking, burning *"witches"* by actually persecuting homosexuals.

Constitutional law has, of course, curbed much of this horror. The question arises whether the constitution will continue to be effective if local majority plebiscites by various persuasions can be allowed capriciously to undo constitutional tenets without Supreme Court review.

It should be made clear that we heterosexuals, who basically in our thinking, do not believe in the persecution of any minorities, are no less troubled, of course, by the biological concept of homosexuality. Indeed we are. But since we have no sound clinical or other authority to prove what biologically or psychologically makes a homosexual inevitable, we have no sane way yet, civically or clinically to deal with the problem. Cruelty, as now being legally practiced, is obviously by any sane standard, the worst panacea for any ill. Destruction of a minority's constitutional rights by local plebiscite is no less than a legally-contorted form of barbarianism.

Psychiatrists, medical science as a whole, along with various persuasions, and the rest of us, so far have come up with only guesses as to what causes homosexuality. We may never know. Persecution, surely, is not a civilized remedy, and is dangerous.

Now that we have become at least sufficiently civilized to keep from unscrupulously throwing homosexuals and intellectual adversaries in jail, perhaps our compassion will become strong enough in time where we will come up with a sane solution to homosexuality; thus giving all people their constitutional rights, prosecuting only those who have been indicted under the law, and persecuting nobody. (Even major criminals have individual rights to a trial by judiciary.)

If we continue the current persecution, the boomerang will only cut us down to the early history's disgraceful level of depravity, where one persuasion presumed the right to legally persecute or slaughter en masse another persuasion.

Perhaps the Supreme Court of the United States will in the end rule whether we should have trial by constitutional law, or constitutional-disenfranchisement of minority elements by local plebiscite.

We are obviously back to that basic premise outlined by the fathers of our country: that for the good of all, church and state must forever remain separate.

Credo: Persecution of minorities is like compressing a spring; both have memories—the recoil becomes as strong as the compression and persecution.

The Public Library

Those who write professionally must live eternally in humble gratitude for public libraries. What makes libraries invaluable is when they are highly functional. What makes them highly functional is not only generous appropriations for the purchase of books, but a staff that is able to bring the overwhelming information a library contains to the reading public, from the youngest reading child on up to the senior citizen.

One gets an idea of the competence required by a librarian when it is realized that every conceivable phase of knowledge that has been documented down through the centuries must be available to the public at the fingertips of the library attendant. While so much is indexed, a vast amount remains buried in limbo, requiring intense probing.

The library attendant is expected to be so well informed it would seem at times, from the complexity of some inquiries, there could be no possible answer, but somehow in the maze of information an answer is found.

When you phone or personally address your problem to the attending librarian and she often comes up with not only an indexed answer, but parts the veils of obscurity for you by an intelligent discussion of the problem itself, one is bound to wonder how such omniscience is acquired.

The big city library is to an advantage broken up in departments where attendants can specialize. The compass of required knowledge by the attendant then doesn't seem so phenomenal. But take the small town library. What you need there is not only one who can steer you to a particular book on a shelf having the subject matter you need, the attendant has to embrace the whole regional group of libraries, and other potential informational centers, to get particular information for you.

And books aren't the whole story. There are visual projection equipment, magazines, clippings, and various other appurtenances to keep us informed and civilized.

Of course, there is a certain erudite employment drift by the educated individual toward the library job, so that we have a commendable lot of capable people working in the libraries, although I wonder if they could ever be adequately paid.

I have often wondered if there would be an auditorium large enough to accommodate a Shakespeare, or other renowned writer, if by magic he could be brought back to address an audience. Yet, the very wisdom that would be spoken in his speech is contained in books—extraordinary, well-documented knowledge that sets on library shelves, ignored by a large part of the population. When I enter a library, I have a feeling of great reverence and intellectual humility for the authors who devoted their lives that the knowledge they conveyed could be made available to us to create a better world.

I see the library of the future a completely revised institution: the librarian, or you yourself, will feed your request into a computer and out will come a list of all the references you require on a subject.

It is just possible that the information you seek will come out in a printed pamphlet or folder for you to keep permanently.

I see libraries of the future with many more chambers for visual equipment where you can see in animation and hear the greats of the past; see in motion past equipment—this also electronically piped to schools from the libraries, so that classes can have before them, the action of the event, as well as the printed word. Professionally read books on tapes are rapidly on the upswing—tapes that can be heard on recorders in cars or at home.

I see miniaturized mechanical, unabridged dictionaries where one doesn't have to page through a tomb to look up the definition and spelling of a word, but merely press a group of syllable-combination buttons.

The tragedy of much of this will be that the machines will be do-it-yourself equipment where the accomplished may not be there to discuss your problem and help you solve it with a smile, generous spirit, and keen mind.

Credo: The library opens up the past, present and future. Enter all these doors for a viable life.

The Censoring and Burning
of Public School Books

On Public Broadcasting, the MacNeil/Lehrer Report carried a program investigating the censoring and burning of public school books. It is that age-old conflict between obscurantism and edification, between Comstockery and enlightenment—again raising its ugly head.

The program reported that even *"The American Heritage Dictionary"* had been banned as obscene—incredible as this seems.

Here obscurantism apparently is on a rampage. It is as though in some of the towns so plagued, book-burning mobs had been loosed on our public schools to reset the curriculum for cultist exploitation.

These censors suggest that by removing the dictionary terms defining the offensive side of life, we will improve its lexicography. This, of course, seems too fatuous to mention. But bear in mind that in this obscurantist censorship we are dealing with a share of Philistinism. It is apparently an effort to keep youth blind to reality—keep them from being whole human beings.

When dealing with an obtuse element it is difficult to convey the psychological fact that where books are publicly censored or burned, as they have been for obscurantist purposes, it is a carte blanche inducement for youth to ferret out duplicate volumes and read them.

If many of the young are thought to be short on some faculties, we can rest assured that *curiosity* is not one of them. They go to libraries to find forbidden books and hide them from their parents under text-book jackets—desirous of knowing what is out there in the real world. Besides having a strong curiosity, they do not as a rule like to be duped and shut out.

Try, if you will, to encompass the vast extent of literature in the world, based on science, art, philosophy, physiology, ethics, the cosmos, accounts of phenomena, and the myriad other subjects that have been challenging the minds of people since the earliest impression on to modern day. Then consider the audacity of the censorious, book-burning element, who notoriously are not readers in the broad cultural sense, presuming to set the edification pattern of the world, by initiating and imposing their narrow choice of literature particularly on youth, and often on adults.

Yet, here they are, we are told, in about 75 towns and cities in the U.S., and pretty much anywhere—where learning is too heavy a burden—presuming to make the big edification decisions of life, only to come up with such historic disgraces of intolerance as the Scopes trial, Comstockery, and other disparagement, and the defaming of their own individual States of the Union forever.

Perhaps one of the worst epidemics of despicable intolerance in the U.S. was that of Comstockery late in the 19th and early in the 20th Century. I quote what a contemporary said, *"The net result of fifty years of Comstockery is complete and ignominious failure. All its gaudy raids and alarms have simply gone for naught."*

Parents who find a diabolic pleasure in book-burning and obscurantist censoring, give the impression that they have a chattel ownership of their offspring, and have a right to shape them any way they please. *Legally* they do have this right. However, where parents are book-burners and censoring obscurantists, it seems deplorable that a pattern of *"like father like son"*, should be permitted to lower the perceptivity of their young. When they carry this into the public square and attempt to destroy the edification of children other than their own, they need to be duly checked.

This, we are told, is one of the penalties of democracy— metaphorically the grain of sand in the pearl, or the so-called fly in the ointment.

Parents shaping their offspring to simulate their own, often narrow adult images, generally leave little hope for any noteworthy professional influence and edification outside of the home. And so we have a multiplicity of mediocre thinking in much youth development and their eventual, consequent emergence into adult Philistinism.

We hear the saying, *"Let me have your child until he is seven years old and you can have him after that."* We have often seen the deplorable result.

Consider for a moment what this implies. The child would, for superior development, have to live under the kindly guidance of a broadly educated, rational, impartial, imaginative, cult-free, non-superstitious foster-parent to be reasonably guarded intellectually and emotionally during the temporal *"seven years"*. How often do you find people in this superior category?

The person who actually made this *"seven years"* statement, wanted his hypothetical *"one-to-seven"* rearing of youth confined to the cult that originated and practiced The Index Expurgatorius. And it is apparently from such cult persuasions that book-burnings have emanated.

Where the young are allowed broad intellectual freedom to

observe the realities of life, seeing—along with its basic amenities—the imposing vexations, afflictions, superstitions, anguish, immorality and cults that beset the young as they grow into adulthood—will the young with a broader education not have a better chance as thinking, free-minded individuals, to make value-judgments and avoid more advantageously the temptations and entrapments of an often lurid world?

Fortunately we do have a share of youngsters coming up in every generation who are courageous and smart enough to decry the Philistine imbecilities of book-burning, and thus prevent much of our highly esteemed, realistic literature from winding up in a colossal pyre of intolerance and stupidity.

Credo: Let not an enforced obscurantism be the deadly disparagement of the young, for they will within a few years of development inherit the earth, and realistically have to come to grips with it.

The Small Town Newspaper

The small-town newspaper is bound to create varied speculation as to its proposals: Is the paper required to be provincial—that is, print largely chatty items about the town's people; or must it also comment on county, state, national and international events?

Some will say that the nearby metropolitan papers give us the wide-range news, and that we had better stick to our own knitting. Others will point out that due to auto transportation the small town, no matter how isolated, can no longer be provincial in scope.

The early-day, small-town newspaper by circumstantial necessity stayed pretty much at home. Aunt Hannah's cooking contribution to the church supper became as significant in the local exchange of town talk as the election of its mayor. If you asked the local carpenter about his political views, he might tell you that he doesn't know much about politics but he can tell you what you want to know about wood. Those, however, were the days without radio or television, when you hitched up Old Dobbin and covered the enormity of a dozen miles a day in a surrey with a fringe on top. We oldsters suffer a little nostalgia about the early life, and try to keep up with the overwhelming change—at times even wondering if the world is going to pot.

High speed transportation and electronic communication have, of course, broadened the scope of the community, so that a small-town newspaper needs to see not only the cultural merit of its essential small talk and local life, but respond to the impending factors of county, state, and nation—even the world as it affects most of us—if it expects more than local attention. Small-town newspapers have on occasion by imaginative and inspiring editors, become nationally circulated, so that some merit is had in trying to make these papers as unique and expansive as possible.

What is likely to keep a small-town newspaper suffering in limbo is that if it gets so hidebound politically one needs to be a card-carrying member of a particular party to get representation. We have seen warnings of this in some newspapers' LETTERS TO THE PRESS section, even in some of the big city papers, where the editor implies that he has the right to determine what letters in substance are to be published. This is treading on editorially thin ice. Public opinion letters can logically and fairly be edited only by the propriety of language—sometimes limited space—but surely not controlled viewpoint, if we are to maintain some semblance of sovereignty by our citizens over imperiousness in government and press.

Editors, on the other hand, do have a certain objective responsibility in keeping local and national life on an ethical track. We saw perhaps the greatest example of this by the Washington Post in the Watergate scandal. It required a great deal of editorial courage; but what, we might ask, has ever been resolved by timidity? The meek inherit nothing.

I have been asked by the publisher of the SUN to write a column. I wrote such a column for the POST MESSENGER of Stillwater in its early heyday under the caption, *"The Outpost"*. Some of the items became a bit explosive, though I was not hung in effigy. But those were more modest days. Can it be that we have come a long, rational way since then, and no longer blush as readily as we used to from reality?

When I first came to the St. Croix River valley in the twenties, it had a growing reputation not only recreationally, but as a cultural center, attracting artists, writers, and other advocates of the arts and crafts. Sinclair Lewis, the great satirist of MAIN STREET and other books, dickered with me for a while to buy some river frontage which I owned, but he finally decided on Lake Superior. We have been fortunate in having enough of an avant-garde in our community to keep the area more cultural and recreational than industrial—a place of peace and serenity. With the River's inclusion into the Wild Rivers program, can we not hope that it will become monumental in the Nation's pride?

Credo: We need to know that the small town paper can spill over into world-wide influence.

The Aspiring Writer

On occasion I get letters from students asking how they might become writers. It seems they are already destined to failure if they have to ask. They had better proclaim an unyielding ambition to do so.

There is a general contention among highly successful writers that one must be born with a natural talent for it, and that it cannot be learned.

But we all have to write. The question is degree, and for what purpose. If it is for strictly utilitarian purposes it can be taught. As to writing for publication it seems that to be a successful writer one needs to have an insatiable desire to write. Then, if one reads and writes with an undaunted spirit, one should succeed. Euphemistically, *"If you take enough baths you will discover that you can float."*

Somewhere back in my reading of history I recall that a political prisoner, an artist, had been deprived of any means to draw. So avid was his interest in art he scratched images on the prison wall with his fingernails. When they wore down and his fingertips began to bleed, he painted pictures with blood.

If I might apply my own theory of gaining some ascendancy in writing, it is to read and write; I repeat, read and write incessantly until one discovers no promising talent for it, or one succeeds.

Such advice as *"perserverance"* sounds a bit too didactic, but I am reminded of the boy who applied for a job in a grocery store. There he found several others looking for the same job. The manager said, *"Here are ten pennies for each of you. Come back tomorrow and the one who throws the largest number of the ten pennies through a dollar-size hole at ten feet gets the job."* One of the boys managed uncannily to throw several pennies into the hole.

The manager asked him how he proved so expert.

Said the boy, *"I practiced all night."*

Some students with a natural aptitude for writing, go through school with professional writing in mind. This, no doubt, is the best complement—a combination of natural talent harnessed to a diligent study of writing rudiments.

I didn't have the good fortune of an academic education since death in my family raised the ugly prospect of poverty. I left school before I reached the end of the seventh grade to help family subsistence.

(This autobiographical sketch is told in my book, *"A Wilderness Autobiography"*, published by the Nodin Press

Inc., Minneapolis, so I wil not repeat it here.) One fundamental point might be worth reconsidering. I continued employment only enough to give me the greatest amount of leisure that could be bought for each dollar earned.

The wilderness cabin offered my greatest economic chance for leisure. There I could read and write for extended periods, while the industrial world ran fitfully on.

I could carry on life as they say, *"on a shoestring"*, then found that the shoestrings laced up golden slippers.

Austerity as generally claimed in the conventional world purports to show disadvantage and underprivilege. One can agree that too often it does. On the other hand, austerity can be the motive power that drives a number of people to success. The difficulty here too often is that the success most sought and frequently achieved is the pecuniary kind. If it gave ultimate fulfillment of life this would be laudable.

We get our best bargain in life when we devote less time and energy in acquiring material needs, and more time and energy in the cultivation of our minds for fulfillment. Intellectual culture cannot be bought. If it could, there would be fewer fools among us.

Universities of late tend to slack up on the humanities in order that people can apply themselves more sedulously to earning money. Are we becoming a nation of well-to-do dunderheads?

Is this not a form of intellectual suicide—a diminishing of life's quality? Metaphorically I am reminded of chickens raised in a poultry propagating factory, where they hatch and live their whole lives out on shelves, as compared symbolically to the eagle that soars over the mountainside observing all.

We need to live optimumly to see what is going on, otherwise we are in a state of dollar anaesthesia.

Our money grubbing lives too often are like travel through a long mountain tunnel. At the far end we see deceptively the alluring light-of-day, where we hope to utilize our monetary gains, only to find when we get there that it was not the morning light-of-life, we had aspired to, but the sunset—no time left to live.

Better, perhaps, that we do not euphemistically take the mercenary short-cut of the unlighted tunnel through life, but the culturally sunlit edifying trail over the mountain. Then, as we reach the valley beyond, we will have lived.

The artist, scientist, writer, and all those who pursue a share of profound values rather than being concerned *alone* with the pecuniary pile, are better equipped, we have seen, to enjoy a degree of euphoric satisfaction throughout life.

The greatest problem is to so regulate life as to enjoy it intensely in youth, middle-age and in the elderly years even though it entails less dollar affluence. One might perhaps assume that if life has had some cultural significance, the fruits would even spill over into posterity—give proof of our having lived magnanimously.

As to the aspiring writer, should we not say, *"Live so that an account of it will not fail to be interesting to others?"*

Credo: We are not remembered by what we have, but what we are. We need to so live and write that we will be worth remembering—have a claim to posterity.

Winter in the North

It is interesting to observe the various attitudes of people toward our Northern winter. The downward dip in the temperature tends to run an equally downward dip in the spirit and vigor of some people. Most everybody except the kids stay indoors.

Winters are too long here at latitude 45, complain many people. At Churchill, on the shore of Hudson Bay, from which place I have taken some wilderness camping trips, one can expect the period from spring-thaw to autumnal frost to be about three months, which should make our summers here at latitude 45, halfway between the North Pole and the Equator, by comparison seem delightfully long.

When the temperature is subzero outdoors and from 65 to 75 indoors, the air indoors is dryer than the desert.

It may seem strange but when the temperature on Hudson Bay dropped to 47 degrees below zero, on a winter camping trip, I suffered most from severe thirst. At that temperature, snow is dry as chalk. Hudson Bay being semi-salt water, the daily task was to melt snow for water, although suspended ice in time leaches out the salt and for melting can replace snow. There is a problem in melting snow for water. A pail filled with snow and placed over a fire allows only the snow in the bottom of the pail to melt. The remaining snow in the pail blots up the water so that the bottom of the pail scorches dry from the fire and gives off a foul flavor to food cooked in it later. The secret is to add snow a little at a time, so that a substantial pool of water forms in the bottom of the pail.

Many people die needlessly in the subzero and blizzard kind of weather. A car far from help can get stalled, finding the occupants subject to severe winter conditions with clothes suitable only to grace a ballroom.

Most important is footwear. If you go from a heated garage in a warm car to some place where only street shoes are worn, security rests on having along in the event of a car stall, a pair of 4-buckle overshoes fitted not to the shoes, but to a combination of wool socks and felt socks. A hooded, down, upper garment (coat or parka), a pair of down pants, and a warm pair of mittens (not gloves) tucked away in the trunk of the car, could save one from losing, by freezing, a foot, hand or even losing one's life. If you are flush with money, add a pair of snowshoes. A few candy bars in the same pack, can add a little metabolic warmth.

Do not use alcoholic liquor for this purpose. It may give you a warm feeling but this is only an anesthesia you are getting, while you freeze sooner.

In the Far North on a winter wilderness camping trip, one wears the following: two-piece wool underwear, two-piece down garment over the wool underwear; for subzero temperatures, wool socks and two pairs of Hudson's Bay Company duffel socks over which go a pair of mukluks—bottoms made of Indian-tanned moosehide (or soft, porous, commercial, split leather) with canvas tops, reaching to just below the knees, held gently snug with a draw cord. (For thawing weather the overshoe combination described earlier is used.) Temperatures in the Far North can go from thawing to 50 below. Over the down under drawers goes a pair of windbreaker pants made of thin, high-count poplin. A parka made of down, pile or fur with a wolverine ruff is pulled (not buttoned or zippered) over the upper part of the body. If wolverine fur is lacking, wolf fur can be used. Snowmobile suits are unsatisfactory because of their lack of convertibility.

Once active on the trail, the parka is removed, just before feeling warm, to avoid perspiration. The less clothes worn without being chilled, the better. Perspiration kills.

It may be of interest to know that intellectual capacity drops in hot weather. Your brain works better in cool to cold climates. There are more and better fish in the cold waters of the world's oceans than in tropical waters. This, for our biological selves, by example, could tell us something.

Comfortably ensconced in a heated house, many people look upon the cold winter weather with a shrug and avoid the outdoors as much as possible. These people might consider that if they took an energetic hike in the cold, they would generate body heat and a feeling of exhilaration where they would have a reluctance to going back indoors. When they do it, they are for the first time getting a grip on optimum health, a keener appetite, better outlook and perception—a change surely for the better.

The North is filled with weather cowards. It is, after all, a case of learning how to live with the cold, an indictment found offensive.

When I met a fellow villager on the street and he said, *"I sure hate this cold weather,"* I answered, *"You need to learn how not to."*

He scowled at me.

Later when I met him he had borrowed from the public library, my book, *"Paradise Below Zero"*. He said in a friendly tone, "I now know what you meant." He dresses differently now, and I see him occasionally on the same route that I hike—not complaining.

There is an old saying that if your feet are cold, put on your hat. Since your whole circulatory system is cooled by exposing any one large part of your body, the suggestion is not far off. Perhaps when people complain about their feet being cold, one might say, *"Use your head"*.

The ulnar and radial arteries, for example, come close to the surface at the wrist. If you wear wool or fur wristlets to cover these points, your fingers will be warmer when they have to be exposed momentarily to the cold.

If I keep on—but enough said—who knows, you might thumb your nose at the annual pilgrimage to California, Arizona, or Florida, and hit at least the local winter trail.

The Northern winter? For hearty men and women. And for men and women who could, if they willed, become hearty.

Credo: If you fail to adapt to the cold—learn how, and dispel incompetence.

Weather

There are only two places in the world, I am told, where the temperature remains about the same the year round. One is the southwest corner of Australia, the other on the Ethiopian Plateau. I understand that the water in southwest Australia is so brackish that life there is untenable.

Whatever the situation in either place, uniformity of temperature cannot be conducive to a better life. We need contrasts.

When spring breaks over the Northland, we who experience it after winter, have a period of euphoria. New growth springing up, bird life breaking into song, rivers and lakes opening to sparkle in the sun, cannot fail to inspire.

Yet, if you reason that all is well, remember that more suicides occur in the spring than in other seasons, and more suicides occur among the affluent than among those not so materially imbued.

It would be a mistake to say that spring gives us the moral and aesthetic lift because we have suffered the *"tortures"* of winter, and find spring a release. This might be true with those who haven't learned how to enjoy winter. I told the story in my book, *Paradise Below Zero,* so I won't expand it here. About mid-winter in a ski competition, 350 skiers passed over a trail through the back of our 5 acre tract, headed up to O'Brien Park on the St. Croix River. They, too, will no doubt enjoy spring when it comes, but perhaps no more than the first substantial snowfall in November.

Lest I repeat what is familiar to some, I ask pardon for the following information which may not be too well understood by others.

The sun in apparent relation to the earth's surface, travels north and south through the year over an arc to a point 23 degrees, 26.4 minutes of arc south of the equator about December 22, called the *Winter Solstice;* and to the same distance north of the equator about June 22, called the *Summer Solstice.*

We use the word *apparent* to note the sun's movement, to explain what it appears and affects to do in its travels over the earth's surface.

The equinox refers to the sun crossing the equator, called the *Vernal Equinox,* when, headed north, it crosses the equator in the spring; and the *Autumnal Equinox,* when, headed south, it crosses in the fall. At those two times of the year, we have an equal amount of daylight and darkness over the earth.

When you reach the higher latitudes—about latitude 66 North—daylight is just about perpetual around June 22, and darkness is just about total around December 22.

As we have winter north of the equator; summer prevails south of the equator, and vice versa.

There is often a certain amount of delusion in tourist travel from south to north in the summer, the theory being that the farther north you go in the heat of the summer, the cooler it will get. We need to remember that the northern sun in mid-summer shines on the earth longer each day than it does farther south, so that in the Far North the earth gets well baked. I have been north of the Arctic Circle and sweltered in the heat, though one can suddenly find the need for warm clothing when the wind shifts and comes down off the icecap and pack ice.

In parts of Alaska, the growth is so increased by the long sunny days, a head of cabbage sometimes can fill a bushel basket.

As we head north in spring on a Canadian or Boundary Waters canoe trip, we'd be wise to check the weather. I've started north from Marine on St. Croix in spring at latitude 45 degrees 12 minutes north, and run into a heavy snowstorm at the boundary waters, less than latitude 50 degrees north. Those coming from the gulf states get even greater surprises.

All is not lost, however, on finding lakes still frozen when you'd hoped to travel by canoe. To watch the spring breakup of the lakes and rivers is an experience you can timewise well afford to see when arriving too early for your canoe trip.

The ice just before the breakup, appears black. One might almost wonder if the lake water, before the breakup, had turned to ink. It is, however, merely the light refraction of millions of ice crystals. Had you cut a cube of ice earlier, it would have appeared to be a solid block of ice. If you attempted to cut out a block just before the breakup, you'd have an armful of ice crystals. The chances are that you will go to bed some evening with the moon shining over a ghostly, black ice surface, only to awaken the next morning to see the sun lighting the whitecaps of a heavily running sea. Mysteriously, the billions of ice crystals are gone, and you are scanning a lake scene where spring has come, and you can now embark on your canoe journey. BON VOYAGE!

Credo: Adjusting to the earth's elements is like reading a profound book—it takes intelligent application.

Hike Back To Health

"Labor-saving device", how benevolent and progressive that phrase has seemed; and yet how insidious. We drive a few blocks to make the most insignificant purchase, and grow fat. We sit on a power-driven mower and grow fat. In short, we use every device we can to prevent using our own physical capabilities when the most essential, healthful, civilizing process in our lives is to keep one's body physically fit, by the flexing of muscles. We are mammalian (animal) not robotistic (mechanical).

Once we are fat the job is to become normal again in stature. Some have tried passive gymnastics, others have tried nostrums, still others have jogged.

Passive gymnastics is a process where a muscular attendant works one's body while one is lying on a table, or, an electrically driven device moves one's limbs.

The nostrums are variable—multifarious beyond belief and worthless.

The jogger neither runs nor hikes. It is something half-way between, but resembling neither. It is a jolting, harmful process.

Passive gymnastic reducing methods are failures. The attendant supplying the passive gymnastics gets the beneficial exercise and a share of your bank account.

The jogger, pounding the pavement with every step, is ruining his feet, endangering his knee and hip joints, and otherwise doing damage to various organs by the impact.

Running adversely to jogging is natural and so is walking. Run, for example, and note the lack of impact. There is a resilience and spring to the step in both running and hiking that does not have the impact jolt of jogging.

Since running is too strenuous for consistent, prolonged exercise, the best exercise by centuries of proof is the hike. It might well be confined to three miles per hour at the start, but in order to get the vigor of needed exercise, the pace, to be physically demanding, should be brought to about four miles per hour.

There are two ways to measure this. Run off the course on a road, perferably a dirt road, with the odometer on your car. Or, buy a pedometer and fasten it to your belt. You can even do this by measured pacing. I normally span 2.2 feet per step. You can use a tape along the ground for say a hundred feet to get an average step length. Since this is not a pace that requires precision, an approximation is good enough.

The longest journey, as the saying goes, begins with a single step. A program of hiking can thus begin with a short jaunt and be increased gradually as one develops an urge to hike substantial distances.

How about a 365 mile hike? Well, you can do this in a year with a mere one mile hike per day, a hike you can do in fifteen minutes. If you hike just under 3 miles per day, something you can do in about forty-five minutes, you will have hiked a total of a thousand miles in a year. Think about that for a moment. The suggestion of a thousand mile hike for anyone is staggering. I repeat, only forty-five minutes each day. The cumulative factor here surprises.

What is interesting about this is that your body is storing up these miles in physical benefit. What do you say such benefit would be to you between the ages of 40 to 50? At less than three miles per day in ten years you would have hiked ten-thousand miles. From 40 to 70, the short daily hike would equal the distance around the world.

The paunch and sparrow legs, if you have them, will be gone the first year.

When you attempt to reduce your weight, may I suggest that you forget nostrums and diet selectivity, and do so by the process of a reduced diet and the hiking mentioned. It has been estimated that one will have to hike 35 miles to take off a pound of fat. This could be discouraging, but don't be fooled by it.

If you walked 35 miles, say over two or three days, and maintained your excess diet, the relative one pound to 35 miles would likely obtain. But cut down one-fourth on your normal intake of food and hike the 35 miles, the distance spread over a period of several days and you will discover a remarkable weight reduction.

That is a reducing formula which won't cost you anything and will work.

I repeat, hike daily and cut down on your food intake. You can eat anything you like if you eat less, not a concern for certain kinds of food, but LESS.

How do you cut down on food without too much discomfort? The fifteen minute period following a reduced meal is the craving period for more food. Once that period is bridged, the craving is greatly reduced. The stomach after fifteen minutes has taken over the process of digestion. It is much like having a bite of food before dinner. As we have been told, *"Don't spoil your dinner."* A smaller dinner when properly handled can thus serve in the same sense to *"spoil"* the overeating of a big dinner, cut out the glut of avoirdupois fatality.

One physician I know tells his reducing patients, *"If you can't cut down on your food intake to keep from getting fat, you have a greater clinical problem than being overweight. Perhaps you should first see a psychiatrist and get your mind in order."*

When one considers the influence of others upon oneself, what a commendable virtue autonomy becomes! To be able to direct one's own destiny to the degree that it can be governed by intellect, what a miracle of advantage we can achieve!

Credo: Fattening of the body may be indicative of *"fattening"* of the brain.

Sensualism Or Higher Achievement?

When one of our early iconoclastic writers pointed out that lower creatures get food, clothing, and shelter; that elementally speaking, too many people do not rise above this status, I presumed that he was referring only to a particular plebeian group. But he spoke more inclusively. He was pointing out that except in prodigious intellectual culture it is only the *sublimation* of food, clothing, and shelter that distinguishes us from lower creatures in the main.

The hungry, he said, seek food of some kind, then aspire to a well-balanced diet, next, to a luxurious diet, and finally on occasion to epicureanism. This ascending scale is true from the poverty level on up to affluence and determines much of the status in society. Thousands of cookbooks are written to titillate the appetite, to make of alimentive sensuality all that can possibly be contributed to it.

The result has been Epicurean in theory, but largely gluttony in practice. We have become a nation of obese people and spend a fabulous fortune annually, about three billion dollars, on methods and nostrums to defat our bodies. Food has become both social pomp and addiction. What we eat, far in excess of what we need, would feed those who die a slow, agonizing terminal death from starvation or undernourishment.

Our closets are packed with clothing that fashionably soon becomes as perishable as unrefrigerated potato salad.

Our homes have gone from the ample, comfortable fireside sanctuary described in classic prose and poetry to the high maintenance, fuel-gobbling structure—a virtual gigantic machine, intended to impress and excite the envy of friends, neighbors, and business associates. In a finite world, this tends toward national resource disaster.

We have viewed glut as propriety, but we might better have looked at it with less myopic vision. If we are of that population, the material and sensual, who begin modestly a level of acquisition, when gained seek the next level of material affluence, then the next, etc., until all of life to the grave is devoted to a higher standard of food, clothing, and shelter as splendor; again I ask, can it be said that we have risen above the basic elementalism of lower animals and have we not failed a possible exalting nobility?

In both a free society and in totalitarian states, the chief concern is apparently with the gross national product, the hope of creating the highest possible material glut. The rise and fall of the stock market can be graphed with how obese our bodies are getting; how large and pretentious our homes are becoming, both to our dismay.

Why are we so incapable of getting rid of the sensual approach and refusing to make at least a feeble effort to grasp the profound values of which there are so many and so available to the open mind?

If we have to decimate our forests, prematurely pump our oil wells dry, suffer from exorbitant, regressive taxes, in order to build, heat and maintain the pretentious home of a white elephant size far beyond our needs, why don't we, in truth, build the structurally adequate, architecturally well-planned home and live without so much panic and stress?

It is simply, of course, that too many people want to impress with little achievement beyond a pretentious ostentatious materialism to distinguish themselves. In the depression of the thirties, thousands, no longer able to accouter themselves with material pretension, jumped through office windows from high-storied buildings, as though escaping from a fire. Materially depleted, the self—the real jewel of possession—was apparently not worth saving.

What has become ironic of late is that so many people with a fairly pretentious pile, trying to boast an impressive contrasting materialism, have culturally become destitute in their search for happiness, when no longer does the pile make the distinction.

Materialistic distinction having largely become outmoded, I suppose that we urgently need a substitute. I don't know what that could possibly be where it would not require intelligent honest cultural effort, since the majority are merely money-grubbing aspirants.

A finite world is suddenly telling us that we need to begin rationalizing our position. Rapidly depleted forests, drying up oil wells, and diminishing mineral deposits might suggest that we get out from behind our irrational way of material glut and face reality. Should this voluptuousness happen to take a turn away from waste and pretentiousness, it ought to have the effect of making us more quality-distinctive individuals. We might even find that a number of people who all along had sought distinction only through material affluence have discovered dormant faculties being aroused enough to make this a culturally better world for themselves and others.

In the February, 1976, issue of *"Readers Digest"* we have a manifestation of what I have alluded to above as a more sensible life. Lawrence S. Rockefeller, brother of the former Vice President during the Ford administration, says, and I quote:

"Some may think it ironic that one who has been blessed with a large measure of material resources should be advocating a simpler life style. Individually, people are finding that a simpler life-style provides greater satisfaction than relentless pursuit of materialism. Americans in growing numbers are finding that satisfaction of material wants does not necessarily bring a sense of lasting well-being. Many long for something which will give a greater sense of purpose and meaning to their lives."

This, I am sure the reader agrees, comes from one so endowed as to speak *"advisedly"*.

Credo: Be not the voluptuary, lest it destroy your body and impoverish your mind.

Vitamins

There will remain a controversy in the clinical arena as well as among the lay population whether we should take vitamins supplementary to our regular diet. Most people shunt this aside with the remark that if you eat a balanced diet you don't need the supplementary pill.

This reminds me of the English teacher who said, *"To do a good job of writing, just express yourself in a simple conversational manner."* To that I answer, *"Where did he get the idea that such a procedure is either simple or easy?"*

I say in the same breath, *"Who, if anyone, gets a fully balanced diet?"* We might add, *"If one has the necessary staples, who prodigiously has the scientific knowledge and the culinary art to keep from committing vegecide in the cooking pot,"* if I may be allowed to coin a term.

Apparently the basic chemistry of vitamins is known, so that they can be synthesized, though the complexity of our biology leaves a number of hypothetical doors open for continuing perpetual research on vitamin chemistry and its effect on us generally.

The Eskimo found the liver of polar bear—as clinical nomenclature would say—*contraindicated* as food, due to its heavy concentration of Vitamin A. It was considered poisonous.

Explorers and long-voyage ship's crews in early days developed the disease *scurvy,* spitting out their teeth from a lack of vitamin C in their diet. Had they known, many of the areas in which they traveled by land, had native rose-hips and other plants containing Vitamin C. Hungarian red pepper has this vitamin in high concentration. When citrus fruits were known to have Vitamin C, limes became a part of the ship's larder, leading to the common expression *"limey"* for the English sailor.

If you are interested in the evolution of Homo sapiens, consider that all animals except man, other primates and guinea pigs, can synthesize in their bodies ascorbic acid, the Vitamin C element. Does this not add one more link of man to his evolution from the primates?

In my earlier wilderness travels in Canada, I came upon a reservation where many of the Indians afflicted with various diseases were preparing to make a canoe journey to a Hudson's Bay Post. The Canadian Government had induced a prominent surgeon and his staff to make a plane flight to the Indian country to examine the health condition of the Indians which had dropped seriously.

The surgeon was averse at his age to undergo a vigorous wilderness journey but government officials assured him that he would have only a hundred-foot hike from the plane landing on the shore to the H.B.C. post buildings and the best of accommodations.

My partner on the canoe trip and I were anxious to see this clinical procedure and its result, so joined the Indian canoe flotilla, giving what aid we could contribute to the most sorely afflicted.

Some Indians were losing their sight, others had great dollar-size, diseased blotches on their bodies, others being even more clinically involved.

Later, my partner and I on our return trip from the wilderness interior, stopped at the post.

The surgeon and his staff were just preparing to leave. A few Indians remained, but they too were readying to leave for the reservation.

The surgeon told me that much of the problem was diet deficiency. The Indians had been buying a great deal of processed, packaged, commercial food. When they lived largely on animal life, a considerable amount of fish and some wild vegetables, there had been few problems of dietary deficiency.

Vilhjalmur Stefansson proved to the medical world that he could live for a year on a strictly meat diet and acquire full vitamin need.

Some time later, I saw a report on the Indian health situation. A vast improvement of the Indians had taken place by administering vitamin supplement pills, fresh meat and staple foods. Blindness had been largely stemmed and the dollar-size sores had pretty well healed.

The Indians were advised to cut back on the processed store foods and go back to much of their native diet.

One of the problems in the store diet was the eating of what became commonly regarded as "dough-gods". The Indians would deep-fry lumps of dough, the brown, crisp doughnut-like dough-gods being especially tasty, particularly when a small portion of the deep-fry fat was butter.

The surgeon told them to substitute dumplings for the deep-fried "dough-gods". When they had boiled their meat, a common method of cooking among Indians, he said, they should use the broth for making dumplings.

One of the Indian patients was a very cute baby boy. The surgeon referred to him as Baby Dumpling. Later at the waterfront I watched the baby's parents readying to depart by canoe for the Reservation. I was so taken by the charm of this youngster I talked a while with the parents, handing them some small gifts of novel items I had picked up at the post. *"What's the baby's name?"*, I asked the mother. She smiled and said, *"Now he is Baby Dumpling"*.

Credo: The balanced diet is largely a misnomer unless you have great dietary competence as cook and clinician.

The Family Physician

Media comment on the recent American Medical Association convention, reveals some startling clinical reappraisals of the family physician's role.

With all the new innovations in clinical hardware and drugs, one might have considered that the emphasis would be here. It wasn't.

Rather than the treatment of major physical breakdowns, the emphasis for one thing was on the maintenance of good health. Doctors were persuaded to urge their patients to pay greater attention to the basic rules of good health: sufficient exercise, enough rest, clean air, good food.

Perhaps this sounds like the old proverbial broken record, but coming from the rostrum of the American Medical Association, it seems almost paradoxically refreshing. Where it had been layman's advice, no matter how valid, it got short shrift.

Another surprise at the convention was that over-specialization was hinted to be on the decline. Twenty-five percent of late medical students have indicated a desire to go into family practice.

We make a mistake if we call this mere caprice of choice. What really is happening here, I think, is that medicine more than ever requires an integrated knowledge of the whole person, biologically and psychologically, for conclusive diagnosis and treatment.

That for a time has apparently been regarded by the profession on the whole as too big a clinical bite for a physician to chew. Thus the tendency toward over-specialization. As the scope of medicine expanded, the study and practice got segmented. It was apparently presumed that the specialist in a particular segment of study would have greater knowledge of that division of medicine than the family physician's general diagnosis and treament.

If we understand the lecturers' speeches at the late convention we must conclude that they were rethinking the position of the family physician. If the family physician was stumped at times in a particular diagnosis, he could always bring in the aid of a specialist.

For several succeeding nights I awoke about 3 a.m. and felt that a microbial war was being fought in my stomach. My physician asked me if I was mentally disturbed over something.

It was a logical question. Mind and guts seem inextricably

intertwined. The family physician is thus more apt to discover what causes a bellyache than the psychiatrist, even though the psychiatrist is believed to know more about psychic matters and their ramified effect anatomically.

The convention also emphasized the importance of the compassionate and sympathetic attitude by the doctor. I have said on entering a doctor's office for clinical help that I would go out the same door I came in, with the same discomfort. This is not always true, of course, and with the filled prescription and clinical advice, one may soon be on the mend.

What one gains from the office call beyond a possible remedy is mental relief, unless, or course, that ailment proves to be fatal. Here in any event, the compassionate and sympathetic attitude of the doctor is a fortifying help.

Though of professional intent, the doctor sitting near the patient with sympathy and compassion, touching, listening with a stethoscope, inquiring, now and then injecting a note of humor, is no doubt one of the noblest of human relationships.

The nurse who can by the same token enter the room of a patient with compassion and sympathy, usually realizes that beyond her more clinical duties she is extending a therapy that supersedes most of what she has learned in materia medica.

If the convention has reexamined and successfully perpetuated the indispensable need for using the intimate rather than the assembly line method in treating the illness of another human being, it may be one of the greatest breakthroughs in medicine, simply by regenerating the family physician, something we once had.

If this could also happen in the general lay treatment of one-another, it could be one of the greatest sociological breakthroughs in history.

Whatever it is that begins at home, surely the compassionate and sympathetic attitude must begin there. We can believe that the individual at the convention who lectured avidly for the doctor's compassion and sympathy, would say that this therapy can work in our homes, offices and on the street as well, before there is need for clinical help—even in some cases, possibly avoid clinical help entirely.

If in the famous words, *"the sun comes up like thunder cross the bay,"* think what a rejuvenation of compassion and sympathy as therapy would sound like if suddenly it were spread over the world.

Credo: Extend a warm hand, a kind word; it will alter the course of mankind for a more tenable existence.

The Cigarette Hazard

The cigarette-smoking death hazard has just been re-emphasized by the Surgeon General of the United States.

How meaningless and unheeded that will be to the average smoker. My wife and I lost five dear friends in just a few years from lung cancer, clinically attributed to the smoking of cigarettes.

All were jubilant people. They laughed when we pleaded with them to stop smoking. They were still quite young—had great plans for the future.

One couple had two beautiful children—a girl about eight and a boy about twelve. The girl seemed to have prodigious musical talent. The boy wanted to be a lawyer—some day run for public office, he said.

Here was precociousness. Here were proud parents.

The future seemed promising. It was the kind of family that aggregatively we can presume would make a great nation.

But the unconsidered factor here was that the father smoked cigarettes. Nothing unusual about that; about sixty million people in the United States smoke cigarettes.

The father had developed a chronic, nagging cough. Nothing unusual about that either, just a way of clearing one's throat, he said.

After much opposition, the mother prevailed; yes, he would see a doctor.

Mother, son and daughter sat it out in the waiting room on three separate occasions, while the father ran the gamut of clincial exploration.

At the end of the sessions the mother was called into the examining surgeon's office. *"I'm afraid,"* he said, *"that your husband has cancer of both lungs."*

An almost paralytic feeling seized the mother. Her children would soon be without a father; she without a very dear husband.

For the kids' sake both parents kept a poker face as they headed for their car at the curb a short distance down the street.

Not a word was spoken. They hoped to make it home before discussing the problem.

As they crossed the narrow strip of turf from the walk to their car, the father stopped. At this moment he became fully aware of the grim, unrelenting fact that a death sentence had just been passed on him. All the glorious plans of the future, a chance to see his kids become distinguished, the thought of his wife having to raise them on her own—all—everything he had worked for, the years of education, gone down the drain. It was a nightmarish cinema racing like mad across his vision.

Standing there on the turf in mortal contemplation, he could not keep his equilibrium. His knees buckled under him, and the next moment he was doubled up on the turf sobbing bitterly, his fists hopelessly beating the turf.

His wife hovered over him, but now she too was down on the turf, her arms around her husband, consumed in tears, the kids in apprehensive terror.

"What's the matter daddy?"

He might have answered this way. *"Many years ago I took an innocent, experimental puff on a cigarette: was that such a terrible offense that I should now be given this death penalty?"*

I remember when cigarettes were called *"coffin nails".* Many firms would not hire a cigarette smoker.

Not being a smoker myself, I suffered from people with foul tobacco breaths. When I met a beautiful girl and later found when kissing her that she had a repulsively foul tobacco breath, *that* ended whatever romance might have developed. Even the power of youthful sex attraction couldn't transcend the stinking breath when one had thought romantically of violets and a wholesome, sweet mouth.

I was surprised in those early days to see women smoke. Fashionably dressed, young, attractive women were smoking in posh restaurants and other affluent gatherings. One wondered if they were not insidiously being subsidized.

When the earlier war against cigarettes was being waged, we heard the same defense: unmitigating denial that cigarettes are harmful.

Following the Surgeon General's finding in January, 1979, as reported in the press, and debated on the MacNeil/Lehrer TV program, we heard the same broken-record lament that cigarettes do not cause lung cancer and heart trouble, though the report stated that now medical science had overwhelming proof that lung cancer takes some four-hundred thousand lives each year, most caused by cigarettes.

Denial gives comfort to the cigarette addict. He or she believes the denial concept up to that clinically crucial moment when the Grim Reaper taps the victim of cigarettes on the shoulder and says, *"Come. I know it is much too early in your life but I have a nice rectangular hole in the ground, bedecked with hot-house flowers, waiting for you."*

There is also another angle to this cigarette-smoking calamity which scarcely ever gets overt consideration: The people who fear a population explosion tell us that the cigarette has been a saving grace over the world for keeping the population in check.

They even claim that the death rate from cigarette smoking improves the quality of the races by killing off the less astute part of the population.

"Would any highly astute individual," they ask, *"knowing the complexity and magnificence of his biological self, and the miracle of mind, choose to erode his body, and impoverish his brain with the known carcinogen effects of cigarettes?"*

I argue that he might if he were a hopeless addict to cigarettes.

They give two factors in answer to this: *"If he were highly astute, would he have been led like a sheep into addiction in the first place, and if he had become addicted, which is unlikely, would he not have the profound sense to quit smoking?"*

Based on this theme of reducing or controlling the population by addiction, to make the world a more viable place to live, should we on meeting the addict, commend him or her by saying, *"Thank you for soon getting out of the way."* Or should we try to salvage those who are not too far gone?

Credo: When you seek help for an addict, remember the appeal is not to the mind but to a form of invalidism.

Is The Future Unpredictable?

Earlier in my life I heard off and on that the world was coming to an end; even documented, specific dates were given for proof.

I was also advised that the world was created in 4004 B.C.

Now, going on my 84th year, I have found that both the cosmic retrospection of the world's incipience and the prognostication of its end, were mere fictional fancies; or, more apparent perhaps, they have been fraudulent perpetrations, asked to be regarded dogmatically as truths.

Science has now found by the carbon 14 and potassium argon dating methods that the world has been in existence many millions of years. And as to *"end-of-the-world"* prognostications, the answer is self-evident; we are still here, and we become aware that there are those who still walk and talk freely among us of things about which they know nothing.

Since both Apocalypse and honest conjecture have fallen flat, science of late has made a desperate effort to predict the future. Most of those presuming to have some sense in this respect, muddle through a mess of apocalyptic jargon along with human apprehension, projection of current life potentials, and come up with a high-sounding pedantry—thus by fooling editors too—get published. It appears edifying. In substance it is usually meaningless.

What, then, can we say about the future where rational minds are contemplating its prospects?

The past incontrovertibly is with us today. If then we consider what science in the past has done socially and ecologically to prepare us for today, we can place little stock in its capability for preparing us for the future.

I do not have the generosity of those who say that scientists have no ethical responsibility beyond innovation and discovery, that they are amoral, not moral. If they do not think and work in the light of contributing to human welfare, and the good of the world as a whole, we can certainly dispense at least with the industrial contribution of science which has made the ecological world a ravaged, polluted scourge.

I hasten to defend those scientists whose aim is to alleviate misery, rather than cause it, if they could possibly need any defense from me.

And if I may extend my egotistical arrogance further, may I suggest to science that the field of social science is still wide open for discovery. Socially we are obviously living in a dark age. And if I may also be permitted to particularize, most of the progress I am sure will be made in ethics, trite as this caveat seems.

Heads of countries, for example, have been lying to heads of countries until the astute have no confidence in written treaties.

The world wracked by fuel problems, has no assurance that the oil industry is not in connivance for exorbitant profits. Lying here has apparently been condoned.

The strange aspect of our problems, whether they be world, country, state, urban or personal is primarily a matter of, I repeat, integrity. This futile plea for honesty is of long standing —something that we usually shed from our conduct as though it were a mere affectation.

And yet, the values of the future will be guided by it. The policing computer eventually will record every *"brownie point"*, every discredit, totalizing our conduct through our lives until the press of a button will reveal whether we are a reputable person, a scoundrel, or of a various shade somewhere between in the ethical spectrum.

The future? All of us will have a computerized biography if we so much as step out of our homes and articulate momentarily with the public. Computers won't be crowded. It will be as though a lifetime biography can be written on a pinhead, and later enlarged to an incriminating or commendatory mountain.

There will be no place on the earth for the scoundrel to hide, and the individual with merit will happily be exposed to the world, to be, we hope, exalted.

What irony! The day will likely come when we can't afford to be anything but honorable in order to survive.

Think then of the individual who has some magnanimity, the person who has by nature or culture, a noble mind, not by mandate of the tell-tale computer, but because he or she is a person of creditable self-determined will, who truly enjoys being competent, decent, and honest.

We might have an asterisk which would mean that an individual is a converted scoundrel in social self-defense, not so by will. That would be revealing.

If we will eventually categorize more particularly, we might arrange people in such divisions as: a life based on greed; subject to superstition; urbanely obsessed; ecologically competent; benevolent; etc., down through the whole gamut of good and bad designations. There will be no place for the scoundrel to hide.

Think what a boon this would be to profile writers—those with only puerile capabilities, who seek realism.

What else can we say about the future? One more thing of possibly many seems evident in controlling our destiny. We apparently are going to run out of energy for a continuing exponential growth: coal, solar energy, deuterium fusion reactors, uranium and thorium breeder reactors, geothermal energy—all have promise but not to the degree of maintaining present exponential growth. In any sense, all but the sun are finite.

Allow me to complement the above energy limitations with a highly speculative but imminent influencing factor for the future. Greatly improved contraceptives, both male and female, will eventually so drastically reduce the populations of the world, as to change all life on earth and its needs. Sex for procreation will become a calculated option. Sex for pleasure will prevail and lose most of its pruderies and oddities. This isn't conjecture—it is rapidly on the upswing now. If you have doubts, pick up your calculator along with reports on geriatrics and childbirth, if you want a surprising computation. Schools are closing in great numbers for want of kids. Millions of lives have been stopped at the existential door.

As to inflation, we need only to wait for the economic bubble to burst. Already we are beginning to reach the point of diminishing returns.

When the economic ball begins to roll down hill, will gravity and despair show up on the graph with the same curve? When we try to rise again, will we proceed to make the same stupid mistakes?

Credo: Since the coming recession was readily predicted, and could have been as readily avoided, we might set it down for future reference as a period of disgraceful avarice in the history of a presumed civilization. May I suggest economic prophylaxis?

Toward A More Tenable Life

No aspect of dissension breeds as much animosity as to consider industrial man's achievements secondary in our cultural, life-quality, hope-of-happiness aspirations. Disparagement of man to express himself materialwise as the ultimate goal is to invite the severest recrimination. Various perceptive groups over the years have on occasion rebuked the idolatry of the smokestack, but none perhaps have so disturbed the sanctity of industrial worship as today's dissenter.

The dissenter, if nothing more, suggests a much needed modification of the establishment's rat race, if we are to give purpose and meaning to our lives. This, of course, seriously threatens to upset industry's long hope of usurping and subduing for profit the whole of man, and disturbs the common tragic illusion that a super-material prosperity could possibly be the basis of happiness in a finite world.

Industry has postulated a plan where we should devote most or our entire lives to fundamental material needs. And once a nominal stage has been achieved, then a higher standard of material affluence, and subsequently still higher, we are told, must be reached. A more leisurely tempo, a liberal education, and substantial periods of healthful life in natural environments are anathema to industry. It disturbs the busy anthill.

Fortunately, we, in a free country, have the personal right to repudiate such tenets. Communism, adopting the same general industrial obsessionism but without the right of individual repudiation, enforces its repressive measures at bayonet point. We in free countries have a choice: the wisdom of revision.

Corrective change is, of course, dreadfully slow; nevertheless, the mind of the minority is beginning to show its effect upon the industrial fanaticism over most of the world. The dissenting effect by our society will for a time be largely psychological since the dissenting element has, so far, manifested no concrete method of resolving some of our ills, and only the obtuse-minded see a safer way of life in totalitarian ideologies. The dissenter has imparted at least a general concept of what he thinks might be hopeful. I cite the following:

1. Get off the industrial treadmill of planned obsolescence and produce only high-quality long-lasting goods. Subvert the machine wholly to man's welfare, not man to the machine.

2. Lay most of the emphasis on individual worth for infinite possibilities of life. Especially decry mass-mind psychology in

any form and regard the totalitarian slave states as a menace.

3. Restore our environment to a healthful state at any cost, for without such action all will eventually be lost.

4. Vastly increase man's leisure, through automation and computerization (if these were intended to have benefits), for his physical and mental welfare. There is a great natural world beyond the city, where life can have a measure of quality. Is it too much then to ask that the city be made viable for life too?

The recent tendency to have holidays so appear as to expand the weekends to three days is an example of hopeful change. A systematic reduction in number of work days is obviously an urgent necessity for both mind and body. We can be quite certain that if, by manipulation of holidays, all are made to appear on Friday or Monday in order to lengthen the weekend, the time will not be far off when every Monday or Friday will be the third day of every work-free weekend. The plan may eventually have the effect also of cutting out not only Monday from the work week but Friday as well—four days each week for escape from the city and its grind could create a whole new happy mode of life. Besides, we can and must do with much longer vacations than the common two weeks, which for mental and physical health should be more like a month twice each year.

Why not? If computerization and automation have proved no value whatever in giving people an increase in health-gaining leisure and diversion to slow down the nervous pace, then these vehicles can have only the alternate effect of burdening us with more rapidly deteriorating industrial junk. The declining number of work hours each day obviously must continue to decline.

Those living within the date of this printing will undoubtedly see a far greater change than the forty hour week. Even now, certain unions are clamoring for a thirty-five hour week. Less nervous pressures and tensions might then begin to reduce the number of beds in psychopathic wards. Labor conflict, racial or otherwise, would have less reason for existing, because all who seek employment would be able to fill in the employment voids created by less work hours. Individual human worth could have greater free expression where the arts and crafts might also conceivably find greater release. Or a man could, to his therapeutic advantage, believe it or not, just sit and whittle, if he chose, while he watched the sun go down over the hills.

None of us should be deceived by the fictitious argument that people will be unable to use the leisure. This has always been an insidious gesture. Life is not that devoid of meaning.

The resourceless and unimaginative would always get help from the resourceful creative element. This anti-leisure propaganda was as fraudulently prevalent when there were no vacations at all in the sixty and seventy-two hour week. *"People wouldn't know what to do with two weeks of idleness,"* we were told. But they did know. Besides, vacation leisure, diversion and fun were turned into a vast multi-billion dollar recreational enterprise. Metaphors are trite, yet the two common ones that *"nature abhors a vacuum,"* and that *"water seeks a level,"* give valuable advice. The many diversionary advantages we have today will more than fill any leisure-created void.

Stewart L. Udall says in the foreword of his book *"Man the Endangered Species", "There is an insidious logic that man must adapt to the machines, not machines to men; that production, speed, novelty, progress at any price must come first and people second; that mechanization must be pushed as far as human endurance will allow. Bigger is not better; slower may be faster; less may well mean more."*

Credo: Time is our greatest poverty. Sell only enough for leisure with security.

Foxfire Books and Their Legend

Where a great diversity of interest is in the physical nature of things, and the craft pertaining thereto is concerned, *"foxfire"* is about as applicable a title as any other appellation, though I can presume that there was a bit of head-scratching before the title *"foxfire"* was finally chosen for these books.

As I understand the project, its inception started with an examination of areas in the country where the simplest devices of a pioneering life were still employed. Austerity has likely had much to do with the continuing use of these early manual devices and methods, but a lot of it, no doubt, resulted from tradition—people accustomed to using simple hand tools and manual methods from generation to generation with satisfaction.

We are beginning to sense irony in the evolutionary process of going from the manual to the mechanization of tools. The sudden diminishing of our oil supply has created almost panic in the modern world, whereas the back country carries on seemingly uninhibited with the manual processes, resorting to power only when industrial invasion has been thrust upon them.

Somewhere, let us say, between disestablishmentarianism and frenzied industry, there has arisen an element of young people who took to the land. They have not been bent on farming in the modern industrial sense but have sought a plot of ground where they could engage in a simple elemental less distressing form of living. I have called on a number of them and would say they are becoming legendary. By the very virtue of their pursuit, they have become a fraternity so extraordinary as to excite the envy of all who are not victimized by convention. A garden, a few chickens, fish from nearby lakes, a hog not stied, a cow, a few hours of outside employment each week, the canning of food; I could go on, but you get the idea. Their minds are at work conceiving that which is largely expeditious to their own elemental life, and they are having just a hell of a lot of fun doing it. They seem to be an intellectual, happy lot.

Intercommunication among them from one part of the country to another, can boast of more articulation, more exchange of idea, I dare say, than any other element in our society. One need only read the Mother Earth publications to discover the fantastic nature of this life. They speak almost a cultural language of their own. Innovation, exchange of idea, expediency— but expediency of reciprocity, accrual to their own peer kind of life. They seem involved in a world of their own, adamant to the frenzied industrial world outside that would suck them into its hurried, nerve-wracking jeopardy if they allowed it.

The Mother Earth people seem the least in jeopardy in a world where mechanization has to spin, race, throb and pound constantly to keep up the artificial tempo. I believe that if all oil wells ran dry, the Mother Earth people would be the most likely to survive, be the least disturbed.

Perhaps my wife and I can speak somewhat advisedly when it comes to comparing the best of two worlds. About half of the year we live on the five acres of wooded land overlooking the St. Croix River described in column one. There we have all the facilities of modern invention, electric power and its incidental appliances. We capriciously press buttons as though there were no *"umbilical cords"* metering the amount to supply our needs. The phone rings and we talk to friends in Alaska, New York, Ontario and locally. A dial would bring an ambulance, the fire department, the police, or whatever. We get almost to the point of taking for granted that these facilities and a thousand others have emanated from the earth as natural attributes. To the degree that they are supplied, to that degree obviously, do we become weaker vessels—more dependent, less capable physically, flabbier, more complex, more under obligation to pay.

But we run from the menace of too much pampering about every six months. Two wilderness retreats await us. One on the shore of Lake Superior when summer's heat gets too enervating. There, even in June, July and August I cut wood from the nearby seemingly inexhaustible forest to keep us warm when the midsummer temperature drops to around 40 on the waterfront. There are no electric buttons to press except for battery operated TV and radio. A dirt road winds pictorially five miles through the Nor'wester Mountains to Highway 61 so that we can avail ourselves of just about anything that money can buy, up to the limit of our fairly ample budget.

Somehow, whether wilfully or inadvertently, we do get plenty of exercise—sometimes to the point where we give a sigh of relief as we tuck ourselves in for the night. It keeps us physically fit.

We are at least elementally on a basis with the Mother Earth people here on Canada's, Lake Superior Shore.

When autumn comes we test our diversionary capabilities and move north of Lake Superior about two hundred miles or more, by car, and a pontoon plane flight. Or, we can go the last measure of distance, when we choose, by canoe and portage.

There on Marchington Lake—a part of the Sturgeon River chain that empties its water into Hudson Bay—we have a base camp. Perhaps there it can be said we go a step or two farther into the more elementary world than the Mother Earth people. Foxfire here seems more appropriate to describe our situation, for it is deep wilderness. And while we live a part of the time comfortably in a cabin, our diversionary travel and living routes are like spokes from the cabin hub.

Today this area is no different from what it was a thousand years ago—having its cyclical change, of course, but still going the full transition circle back to where it has been primordially through the ages.

Credo: Foxfire; could we not see it as a symbol from which to draw something vitally inspiring from our environment?

Guru

Some time ago the St. Paul Sunday Pioneer Press-Dispatch in giving me a two-page spread on my writing program, referred to me as a Guru. I was only vaguely familiar with the term, so consulted Webster. The term was a bit flattering if I took seriously the dictionary definition that a guru is *"a charismatic leader or guide."*

The common presumption is that when one becomes a mentally active senior citizen, a retrospective glance at one's own life should conjure up a few answers to life's problems for the younger element to consider. I asked a 95-year-old man if he had any basic thought to pass on to the young. He said, *"Life is 100 percent trouble but 98 percent never happens."* The individual who can discover the needless apprehensions dogging us daily so as not to worry himself through life with a batch of ulcers and a coronary, is likely the exception. And it may be just as exceptional to find the young ever accepting advice from elders. Somehow the young have to perpetually repeat the same basic mistakes in order to gain maturity. To suggest that the young should hope to bypass the most obvious, common mistakes, and thus save half a lifetime of wasted hours, is generally futile advice. Now and then, but with great rarity, a prodigious youngster does see the folly and avoids much trouble, but the hazard here is that with self-esteem (and I mustn't forget sex), dominating our every move, most of us think we possess the required critical analysis, when we don't.

A young, enterprising man employed by a large firm was being considered for an assistant executive post. He was thoroughly investigated and found to have an impeccable record of honesty and forthrightness. After the investigation a personnel manager came to see him. To entertain the manager, he was taken on a fishing trip by the young executive-aspirant, who drove 75 miles per hour instead of the 55 mile requirement. At the end of the trip the personnel manager said, *"The investigation shows you to be a person of fine character, but anyone who drives 75 miles per hour in a 55 mile zone, lacks the good judgment we need for our executives."*

When we see people throwing beer cans out onto the highway, can we not assume that they would not have the responsibility for holding important jobs, or be trusted with company or public cash; even when employed in a lowly position, be expected to give an honest day's work. (There is also risk here of the criminal mind.)

When a president, and what turn out to be his henchmen, become dishonest scoundrels, how does a parent or a *"guru"* tell the young that good character still pays off? It definitely does, you know. The more common dishonesty that prevails, the greater will be the demand for people of integrity at higher salaries. We need to beat the bushes to find these upright individuals.

They, and their accomplishments, will be the only hope of viably preserving the world.

Credo: Maintaining integrity among many scoundrels is difficult, but it is the power that endures and achieves results.

My Urban Renewal

One day recently, my wife and I left our outer-suburban home on the St. Croix River and visited the Twin Cities, Minneapolis and St. Paul. It was her first visit after a lapse of eighteen months, mine after a lapse of several years.

When it is considered that I was raised in the Twin Cities, that I spent a substantial part of my adulthood there, would you be surprised if I told you that it seemed as unfamiliar to me as though I were in Paris or London where I have never been?

The visit in more ways than a chronological re-evaluation of a city was a gala occasion, in that my latest publisher brought us from the St. Croix in the morning and returned us in the evening. We dined at his club, had a tour of his whole establishment and the loop of Minneapolis.

If this does not seem anomalous, consider that I have had contact with New York publishers for a number of decades, and at times considered it an achievement to reach them for a few brief remarks on the telephone. Moreover, after eight books of mine published in New York, I have not met any of the editors in person, nor their agents who worked in this territory.

Perhaps the day will come when one will get only a phone connection with a publisher's computer in New York, to clear up a thing or two in the publishing process of one's books.

As the writer of a number of books on wilderness, I have on rare occasions, however, had editors bring their office to a screeching halt while they momentarily exchanged a word or two on the phone about their own outdoor interest.

I would like to see editors and writers in strong rapport for better books and a better world.

New York editors seem estranged and captive.

Not so my aforementioned publisher and editor. He seems to have the organizational talent to keep his business going so that he can enjoy and clinically benefit from a cabin in the wilds. When the pressures get too great, he is off to the Silent Places of the lake and forest country in the North, or he flies to some foreign country where phones can't readily reach him.

If we do not think this is paradox, how many executives do we know who do it, who do not suffer mental anguish when they are not present for the opening of the morning mail?

As we sat dining in the club of my publisher, looking out over the city, I saw a twelve-story building being dismantled to provide a lot for a modern structure. Earlier in life I saw that twelve-story building being erected. Now at age 84 I was to see it leveled.

It was festooned with elaborate stone arches over windows, an imposing stone-carved entranceway, while gargoyles emblazoned its roof spouts—sentinels that had stood the watch of a half century or more.

Were these to be preserved by the wreckers? Not in the petulant high-labor-cost age. A ball weighing a ton dangling from the arm of a huge crane, would be swung to batter into rubble what was once the architectural achievement of artisans and craftsmen.

The nostalgia and sentiment I had for the things of old seemed no less battered into rubble. I thought of that tearful group who saw a centuries-old redwood tree reduced to lumber.

I was amazed by the routes from building to building through skyways, where one can remain indoors and still cover much of the loop.

I have heard of people in New York going about the city in subways and skyways, living their lives scarcely ever seeing the sun or a green bit of growth. From the cosmetic counters they simulate a glow of health in their cheeks.

I am reminded of pocket gophers that live underground, moving through tunnels, feeding on roots and tubers. The people hiking through skyways were likewise going from counter to counter foraging for what they needed.

My autograph desk and chair were situated near the entranceway of the bookstore, a rather substantial segment of a large department store.

On long, early wilderness journeys I had set my fishnet at narrowing outlets. Near the bookstore entranceway I was presumed to catch the flow of pedestrians.

At first a single pedestrian would stop and flash the pages of a book then quickly move on. When two or more stopped it attracted others, until a crowd formed and I found myself addressing an audience. The autographing routine became mixed with answering questions, trying to hold the interest of the crowd and personalize each sale and autograph. I became the chautauqua salesman, remotely the writer.

I have often thought that the writing of books was enough, and that publishers would sell one's book, but it seems that appearances by an author are highly essential. There is apparently some kind of magic in the autograph, in the image-shaping of the author by the reader.

"My husband is a great fan of yours," are words an author likes to hear. When the lady says, *"I am sorry he isn't here to meet you, but he will be surprised when I tell him that I met you,"* one realizes the importance of the flesh and blood com-

plement that authors need to have with their books.

Yet, I wonder sometimes if the legendary image that one's readers have conjured up in their minds, is not the better one over reality. When in their minds they have a masterful figure of great charisma constructed, should that not be left, rather than suffer the illusion of reality?

Credo: Read books to acquire existential clues, but be your own guide through life.

In Conclusion

At my age, 84, I am still optimistic about the future world. I say this , of course, with the reservation of having to face the imminence of some currently threatening and degrading forces apparent to all of us.

I have come to believe that we are entering into an encouraging era when the detrimental effects of industrialization will begin to diminish. The need for placing cultural values above an obsessed materialism is slowly inching its way into recognition. Man-for-the-machine is gradually giving way to machine-for-the-man—a machine that does not imperil the safety of man beyond his own negligence, but expedites as well his lot for better living and leisure. Here more consideration is being given at last to foolproofing, to safety factors of required mechanical redundancy.

Also entering the scene is a new scientific rebellion. It is not only the college-student-groups, and other lay population, who of late are protesting industrial obtrusion upon human values, health and existential viability, but the advent of knowledgeable scientists—people who know as much or more about the imposing industrial hazards as the agents of industry themselves. For want of a better term they have been called by some, *"techno-rebels."*

In the field of bio-technology, the techno-rebels have gone so far as to attempt predetermining the advisability of further research, lest we release a genie from the bottle that will destroy most of mankind.

But here, if ever there was mootness to consider, is a question great as any we have faced. It may be in the bio-technical puzzle where serious consequences are apparent, but it may also be here that we have the means of resolving some of our greatest problems.

It is here where adventurous research most challenges the scientist, and where there is need for the largest budget risk to augment it.

Perhaps we have been making the mistake that most basic areas of science have already been explored and that we are now merely in the refining process. Recently discovered phenomena dispel that notion, of course.

We now face potentials so great, it seems we have, to date by comparison, just skimmed lightly over the possibilities that exist. Hypothesis is elbowing its way through false presumption of past accomplishment. The back trail of achievement seems to offer less criteria than ever for the future.

We have been too busy mechanizing to be conscious of the most important need in life: preservation of human values. The machine has been too fascinating to really discover its appropriate need and application to life. It became a fetish, a dangerous toy, poorly handled in so many instances.

That is gradually changing as we look retrospectively at the ensuing, mounting junk pile. The car no longer is a status symbol. We now see it largely as expedient mobility at a price we can afford to pay, and if we can pay there is a question whether we will permanently have the fuel to keep it operating.

I think we are discovering that we have been carrying on life too petulantly, too attritionally, too extravagantly. Our bodies won't tolerate the psychotic disturbance and wear. We need to slow the pace.

The finite nature of materials has been reduced already to show that the pace of material consumption as well needs to be drastically cut down. This is not privation; it is likely to be more expeditious to life's values. This can be explained only by recognition of such values, not only material cost. The value of wise economy is gradually being discovered as a life-giving force. The lesser ration of food is for most of us nutritionally better assimilated. The less we drive and the more we walk become increasingly conducive to our well-being.

These gradually emerging rediscoveries, becoming more apparent, are what give me that sustaining optimism about the future.

We are told that we should go back to the more elemental life we lived in early days. What seems more plausible is that we might take advantage of modern achievement in such a fashion as to choose value-inducing, beneficial factors rather than mire ourselves in a material-imposing glut. Practice wise discretion, that is, in the midst of plethoric temptation.

I believe that we are gradually coming to that. The tragedy would be if we do not try to accomplish what we can now. I would hate to think that if we fed the particulars of wise living into a computer it would tell us that only in some far-distant future will we become civilized enough to learn how best to live.